SEXUALITY

Sexuality is as much a product of culture as it is of nature. It is not simply a matter of biological or psychological 'drives' or of genetic imprinting. The most important sexual organ is between our ears. Sexuality has both a history and a sociology. Drawing on a range of theoretical approaches, including the analysis of Michel Foucault, *Sexuality* provides an indispensable, comprehensive introduction to the social and cultural understanding of sexuality, discussing its cultural and socio-historic construction, its relationship with power, and the state's involvement in its rationalization and regulation.

This fully revised edition brings the debates up to the present, and examines the subjects in terms of contemporary social, moral and political issues, and features new material on AIDS, queer theory and the influence of postcolonial theory on the study of sexuality. This new edition confirms the classic status of the book, and engages with the central issues for our understanding of sexual life.

Jeffrey Weeks is Executive Dean of the Faculty of Arts and Human Sciences at London South Bank University.

KEY IDEAS

Series Editor: PETER HAMILTON, The Open University, Milton Keynes

Designed to complement the successful *Key Sociologists*, this series covers the main concepts, issues, debates, and controversies in sociology and the social sciences. The series aims to provide authoritative essays on central topics of social science, such as community, power, work, sexuality, inequality, benefits and ideology, class, family, etc. Books adopt a strong individual 'line' constituting original essays rather than literary surveys, and form lively and original treatments of their subject matter. The books will be useful to students and teachers of sociology, political science, economics, psychology, philosophy, and geography.

Citizenship
KEITH FAULKS

Class
STEPHEN EDGELL

Community
GERARD DELANTY

Consumption
ROBERT BOCOCK

Culture
CHRIS JENKS

Globalization – second edition
MALCOLM WATERS

Lifestyle
DAVID CHANEY

Mass Media
PIERRE SORLIN

Moral Panics
KENNETH THOMPSON

Old Age
JOHN VINCENT

Postmodernity
BARRY SMART

Racism – second edition
ROBERT MILES AND
MALCOLM BROWN

Risk
DEBORAH LUPTON

Sexuality – second edition
JEFFREY WEEKS

Social Capital
JOHN FIELD

Transgression
CHRIS JENKS

The Virtual
ROB SHIELDS

SEXUALITY

SECOND EDITION

Jeffrey Weeks

Routledge
Taylor & Francis Group

LONDON AND NEW YORK

First published in 1986 by Ellis Horwood Ltd
and Tavistock Publications Ltd

Second edition first published 2003 by Routledge
11 New Fetter Lane, London, EC4P 4EE

Reprinted 2004

Simultaneously published in the USA and Canada
by Routledge
29 West 35th Street, New York, NY 10001

Routledge is an imprint of the Taylor & Francis Group

© 1986 and 2003 Jeffrey Weeks

Typeset in Garamond and Scala Sans by Keystroke,
Jacaranda Lodge, Wolverhampton
Printed and bound in Great Britain by
TJ International Ltd, Padstow, Cornwall

British Library Cataloguing in Publication Data
A catalogue record for this book is available from the British Library

Library of Congress Cataloging in Publication Data
Weeks, Jeffrey, 1945–
    Sexuality/Jeffrey Weeks.—2nd ed.
        p. cm.—(Key ideas)
    Includes bibliographical references and index.
    1. Sex. 2. Sex customs. I. Title. II. Series.
    HQ21.W379 2003
    306.7—dc21   2003007360

ISBN 0–415–28285–3 (hbk)
ISBN 0–415–28286–1 (pbk)

Contents

Editor's foreword to the first edition

We are, as Jeffrey Weeks points out in this book, almost programmed into thinking of our sexuality as a wholly natural feature of life. It is of course a truism that sexual relations are but one form of social relations, but we are nonetheless accustomed to think also of social relations as 'natural', at least in the commonsense world. Yet it is the task of sociology and the other social sciences to 'deconstruct' naturalism, and to determine how actions are given their meaning and significance via social interaction. Why in principle should not sexuality be treated as socially conditioned a phenomenon as, say, chess-playing or cuisine? The liberationist philosophies of the post-war generation have accustomed us to a search for a 'natural' and unrepressed sexuality, as if there were at bottom some essential form of sexual relations whose expression lies in an extra-moral domain. Yet simultaneously the same generation has also been the site of a resurgence of homosexuality, of transvestism, of pederasty, and of fierce and critical debate about the negotiation of gender identity. As the philosopher–historian Michel Foucault pointed out, sexuality is no more (or no less) than a historical construct. Its meaning and expression is no wider or extensive than its specific social or historical manifestations, and explaining its forms and variations cannot be accomplished without examining and explaining the context in which they are located.

Jeffrey Weeks has written extensively on what we might call the new sociology of sexuality, and is representative of the way in which what was a slightly 'marginal' academic interest has come to full respectability. It is slightly ironic that sexuality should appear to have increased its hold over aspects of popular culture (cf. the mass of sexual media currently available in Western societies and the ubiquity of sexual imagery in advertising) at the same time as the new perspectives on sexuality attempt to deconstruct it as a cultural expression. However, our preoccupation with sexuality does mean that it is more necessary than ever to interpret and elucidate this all-pervasive ideology.

One important feature of the present interest in sexuality is its linkage with a parallel concern with questions of family, kinship and household organization. The massive expansion of 'family history' as a site of academic research, has itself more empiric parallels in the growth of social policy initiatives, social intervention in the lives of families, indeed the emergence of a field of bio-politics in which the state can be seen as attempting to regulate and control. Both psychological and social therapies devote great attention to the sexual dimension of their clients' lives. This is not perhaps an entirely new feature of social control, for the Church and the village community were at least as concerned about regulating and organizing sexual behaviour in Western societies of the pre-industrial era, as is the modern state. But what is different and qualitatively new is the attention paid to the rationalization of sexuality, and its subjection to scientific study, in modern Western society.

In the detailed and carefully argued discussion of the sociology of sexuality which Jeffrey Weeks has written, the connection of sexuality to its socio-historical context is explored in ways which reveal just how completely sex is socially constructed. This naturally raises problems about sexual morality which are likely to cause a certain amount of unease. For if sexuality is at base a social convention of almost infinite variety, then nothing is either 'right' or 'wrong'. Clearly – as Weeks is concerned to stress – the issue cannot be left there. We are rational and intelligent beings who have the capacity to choose the moral codes under which we live – or at least to negotiate modifications and adaptations to them.

Peter Hamilton

AUTHOR'S PREFACE TO THE SECOND EDITION

This short book has in a sense been my intellectual manifesto. It summarizes a debate, and my position in that. But nothing stops still. It is now some eighteen years since I completed the first edition of this book, and a great deal has happened to me, and the world of sexuality. The book has been happily in print throughout that period. It has been translated into Spanish and Japanese as a whole, and sections have appeared in a variety of other languages. My views have not changed fundamentally since the book was first published. But the scholarship of sexuality has experienced a transformation. What seemed an esoteric subject for a historian and sociologist in the 1980s, has now become a mainstream topic, taught in all universities across the Western world and beyond. There has been a mountain of new research, and a continent of publications. It seemed time, therefore, to look again at *Sexuality* to see whether it was fit for purpose for new readers in the twenty-first century.

When my editor approached me to do a new edition, I confess I hesitated. On the one hand, the essay on sexuality that I wrote in the mid-1980s had a certain integrity, reflecting the passions, preoccupations and priorities of the time in which it was written. As such, I am told, it had achieved a sort of classic status, and I am deeply grateful for all those readers who have contributed to that. I was reluctant to change a dot or comma. On the other hand, there is no point in keeping what was intended as an active intervention in contemporary debates in a deep freeze while the world moves on. Many of the issues that engaged me in the 1980s are still live; new issues have emerged, on which I have strong opinions. I believe the approaches I put forward in the 1980s still have relevance to an understanding of the present. But they needed refreshing by taking account of the new scholarship. So I allowed myself to be persuaded that a new edition was indeed needed. This is the result.

The structure of this new edition remains broadly the same as in the first edition. But within that structure I have taken the opportunity to rewrite and update every chapter, both to amplify my arguments as necessary, and to take into account the changes both in the world, and in the literature which tries to understand it. The book is therefore about a third longer again than the first edition. But it remains, I hope, true to my original intentions, and a concise guide to the debates about the history and social organization of sexuality. The interested reader can follow through my own views in the other books I have written on sexuality and intimacy, which are listed in the suggestions for further reading. I have also tried in that section to reflect a broad selection of other work. One of the arguments of the book is that sexuality is in part being shaped and reshaped by the ways in which we think and write about it. This book represents part of my own contribution to that necessary process.

Jeffrey Weeks
London 2003

Acknowledgements to the First Edition

It is now over ten years since I first began writing on the history and sociology of sex. During that time I have incurred many intellectual and emotional debts. There is no space here to record the names of all the people who have helped me. I refer readers to the acknowledgements in my previous books, full details of which are given in 'Suggestions for further reading' at the end of this book. All I can do here is to thank them all once again, and to free them from any obligation to agree with everything (or anything) I say here.

Some debts are immediate, however. I must thank Peter Hamilton for asking me to write this book, Caradoc King for encouraging me to do so, Barbara Giddins for patiently transferring my early drafts into legible type which allowed me to rethink, rejig and rewrite, and Janet Hussein for (as ever) typing an impeccable final draft. My gratitude, as always, goes to Chetan Bhatt, Micky Burbidge and Angus Suttie for sustaining me during its writing. But my greatest debt is to my students, whose questions, doubts, anxieties and stimulation have forced me to think through many of the issues I tackle here. I therefore dedicate this book to my students – past, present and (government policy permitting) future. I hope they get as much from this essay as I got from them.

ACKNOWLEDGEMENTS TO THE SECOND EDITION

My debts to other writers and to many more generations of students continue to grow. I hope I have done them justice in this new edition. I want particularly to thank my colleagues at London South Bank University for their support as I have tried to combine writing about sexuality with increasing managerial responsibilities. I owe a special debt to the following: Ros Edwards, Clare Farquhar, Philip Gatter, Brian Heaphy, Janet Holland, Rachel Thomson, Matthew Waites.

Sadly, a number of friends and colleagues who supported me in various ways as I wrote the first edition have since died. I still miss and mourn them, especially Angus Suttie.

My greatest debt is to Mark McNestry. I can simply thank him for everything.

1

THE LANGUAGES OF SEX

> Sex is an either/or phenomenon – appealing or appalling, rarely in
> between.
>
> Murray S. Davis (1983: 87)

The more expert we become in talking about sexuality, the greater
the difficulties we seem to encounter in trying to understand it. Despite
sustained attempts over many years to 'demystify' sex, and several decades
of much proclaimed – or condemned – 'liberalism' and 'permissiveness',
at least in the West, the erotic still arouses acute moral anxiety and
confusion amongst many people, not least the guardians of our morals.
This is not because sex is intrinsically 'naughty', as a sensitive commen-
tator has rightly remarked, but 'because it is a focus for powerful feelings'
(Cartledge 1983: 170). The strong emotions it undoubtedly arouses gives
to the world of sexuality a seismic sensitivity making it a transmission
belt for a wide variety of needs and desires: for love and anger, tenderness
and aggression, intimacy and adventure, romance and predatoriness,
pleasure and pain, empathy and power. We experience the erotic very
subjectively.

At the same time, the very mobility of sexuality, its chameleon–
like ability to take many guises and forms, so that what for one might
be a source of warmth and attraction, for another might be one of

fear and hate, makes it a peculiarly sensitive conductor of cultural influences, and hence of social and political divisions. Not surprisingly, therefore, especially since the nineteenth century, sexuality has become the focus of fierce ethical and political divisions: between traditional moralists (of various religious hues, or of none) and liberals, between the high priests of sexual restraint and the advocates of sexual liberation, between the defenders of male privilege and those such as feminists who challenged it, and between the forces of moral regulation – the upholders of 'traditional values' – and a host of radical sexual oppositions, some of whom attack each other as much as they oppose sexual orthodoxy.

In the past such debates might have been regarded as marginal to the mainstream of political life, whatever their importance for those closely involved. Increasingly over the past decades, however, sexual issues have moved closer to the centre of political concerns. In North America and Europe the 'New Right' from the 1980s mobilized considerable political energies through its emphasis on the so-called 'social issues': an affirmation of the sanctity of family life, hostility to homosexuality and 'sexual deviance', opposition to sex education, and the reassertion of traditional demarcations between the sexes; all have proved powerful weapons in building new political constituencies for conservative politics. On a global scale, so-called 'fundamentalists', whether Christian, Islamic, Jewish or Hindu, or of no settled religion, have placed the body and its pleasures at the centre of their efforts to draw the curtain on the failures of the present and to go back to the future by reconstructing neo-traditional societies, marked by rigid distinctions between men and women, the harsh punishment of transgressors, and a bitter rejection of Western secularism. All this in turn can be read as a back-handed compliment to the entrenchment of certain liberal values of autonomy and choice, and the success of feminism and radical sexual movements, like the lesbian and gay movement, in challenging many of the received norms of sexual behaviour, identities and relationships. 'Progressive opinion' in the West may not at first have quite known how to react to these challenges but there is now a widespread recognition that the ground rules of the debate have irreversibly shifted. So much is clear. What is less apparent is how we are to negotiate our way through the maze that apparently constitutes 'sexuality', especially as we enter a world of 'global sex'.

In the West, at least, sexuality has been seen as having a special relationship with the nature of virtue and truth since before the triumph of Christianity. Through our sexualities we are expected to find ourselves and our place in the world. What was mooted in the debates of late antiquity, codified by the early Christian disquisitions on the flesh and personalized in the procedures of the Catholic confessional and Protestant witness before God, reached an apotheosis in the nineteenth century as medicine and psychology, sexology and pedagogy, took on a role, alongside the Churches, of establishing moral and social standards. By the end of the nineteenth century, as many observed, doctors had adopted some of the attributes of a new priesthood, and many of its members seemed as certain of their views as the old. But the increasing politicization of sex in the past century or so offers new possibilities and consequent challenges: not just of moral control, and its inevitable converse, sexual transgression, but of political analysis, opposition and of change. This makes it all the more necessary that we know what we are talking about when we speak of sexuality, that we clarify the meaning (or more accurately meanings) of this complex phenomenon. We need to know what it has been and is, before we can rationally decide what it should, or could, be.

This is an easy aim to proclaim. It is a notoriously more hazardous task to carry out. All of us have so much invested in our own concept of what is the 'true sex' that we find it difficult enough to understand dispassionately the sexual needs and behaviour of our closest contemporaries, let alone the infinitely more ambiguous desires of our predecessors. The mists of time and the various disguises of prejudice conveniently obscure other ways of living a sexual life, and the merits of diverse sexual cultures. This resilient will-not-to-know is backed up by an assumption which is deeply embedded in perhaps all our cultures, but strongly in the West: that our sexuality is the most spontaneously natural thing about us. It is the basis for some of our most passionate feelings and commitments. Through it, we experience ourselves as real people; it gives us our identities, our sense of self, as men and women, as heterosexual and homosexual, 'normal' or 'abnormal', 'natural' or 'unnatural'. Sex has become, as the French philosopher Michel Foucault famously put it, 'the truth of our being' (Foucault 1979). But what is this 'truth'? And on what basis can we call something 'natural' or 'unnatural'? Who has the right to lay down the laws of sex? Sex may be 'spontaneous' and 'natural'. But it has not stopped an endless barrage of advice on how best to do it.

Let us start with the term 'sex' and its common uses. Its very ambiguity signals the difficulty. We learn very early on from many sources that 'natural' sex is what takes place with members of the 'opposite sex'. 'Sex' between people of the 'same sex' is therefore, by definition, 'unnatural'. So much has usually been taken for granted. But the multiple meanings of the word 'sex' in these last few sentences should alert us to the real complexity of the question. The term refers both to an act and to a category of person, to a practice and to a gender. Modern culture has assumed an intimate connection between the fact of being biologically male or female (that is, having appropriate sex organs and reproductive potentialities) and the correct form of erotic behaviour (usually genital intercourse between men and women). The earliest usage of the term 'sex', in the sixteenth century, referred precisely to the division of humanity into the male section and the female section (that is, to differences of what later was called gender). This eventually gave rise to the idea that 'sex' is the basic biological datum on which the cultural and social divides of gender are built. The other dominant meaning today, and one current since the early nineteenth century, refers to physical relations between these polarized sexes, 'to have sex'. The word sexuality (the abstract noun referring to the quality of being 'sexual') developed its modern meanings in the second half of the nineteenth century, and came to mean the personalized sexual feelings that distinguished one person from another (*my* sexuality), while hinting at that mysterious essence that attracts us to each other [1].

The social processes through which these mutations of meaning have taken place are complex. But the implications are clear, for they are ones we still live with, even as they are questioned, demystified or deconstructed. In the first place, there is a continuing assumption of a sharp distinction and polarization between 'the sexes', a dichotomy of interests, even an antagonism ('the battle of the sexes') which can only be precariously bridged. Men are men and women women – and this is truth embodied in the dominant structures of heterosexuality, from which everything else remains a falling away. Secondly, there is a belief that 'sex' is an overpowering natural force, a 'biological imperative' mysteriously located in the genitals (especially the wayward male organs) that sweeps all before it (at least if you are male) like hamlets before an avalanche and that somehow bridges this divide, like a rainbow over a chasm. Thirdly, this gives rise to a pyramidical model of sex, to a sexual hierarchy stretching downwards from the apparently Nature-endowed correctness of heterosexual genital intercourse to the bizarre manifestations of 'the perverse', hopefully safely buried at the base but unfortunately always erupting in dubious places.

Much has changed during the past few generations. We are much more tolerant of difference. There has been a re-evaluation of the relationships between men and women. But this view of the world of sex remains deeply embedded in our culture, part of the air we breathe. It still provides an ideological justification for uncontrollable male lust, and even, therefore, for the fact of rape and violence, for the downgrading of female sexual autonomy, and for the way we treat those sexual minorities who are different from ourselves, as well as for the more acceptable verities of love, relationships and security. Since the late nineteenth century, moreover, this approach has had the ostensibly scientific endorsement of the broad tradition known as sexology, the 'science of desire'. Sexologists such as Richard von Krafft-Ebing, Havelock Ellis, Auguste Forel, Magnus Hirschfeld, Sigmund Freud and many others, sought to discover the true meaning of sex by exploring its various guises: the experience of infantile sexuality, relations between the sexes, the influence of the 'germ plasm', the hormones and chromosomes, the nature of the 'sexual instinct', and the causes of sexual perversions. They often disagreed with one another; they frequently contradicted themselves. In the end, even the most dedicated had to admit to a certain defeat. Freud confessed to the difficulty of agreeing 'any generally recognized criterion of the sexual nature of a process' (Freud 1916–17: 323), and although today we may claim to be a little more confident in knowing what is 'sexual' or not, we are still in as much of a fog as those pioneers in interpreting its implications. The revolution in genetics we are now living through, in its mapping of DNA, its search for the genes for this attribute or another (the 'gay gene' being perhaps the most notorious), has not fundamentally challenged, has in fact often confirmed, the difficulties and perils of this endless quest to understand the mysteries of sex.

Sexology has had important positive effects in extending our knowledge of sexual behaviours and I have no desire to denigrate its real achievements. Without it we would be enslaved to an even greater extent than we are to myths and nostrums. On the other hand, in its search for the 'true' meaning of sex, in its intense interrogation of sexual difference, and in its obsessive categorization of sexual perversities it has contributed to the codification of a 'sexual tradition', a more or less coherent body of assumptions, beliefs, prejudices, rules, methods of investigation and forms of moral regulation, which still shape the way we live our sexualities. Is sex threatening and dangerous? If we want to believe that then we can find justification not only in a particular Christian tradition but in the writings also of the founding fathers of sexology, and in many of their scientific successors. Is sex, on the other hand, a source of potential freedom, whose liberatory power is only blocked by the regressive force of a corrupt civilization ('beneath the cobblestones the beach' as the student revolt in Paris, 1968, headily proclaimed)? If so, then justification can again be found in works of polemicists and 'scientists' from the nineteenth century to the present, embracing not only socialist pioneers such as Charles Fourier and Edward Carpenter, Freudo-Marxists like Wilhelm Reich and Herbert Marcuse, but also more ostensibly sober-suited 'social bookkeepers' like Alfred Kinsey. Whatever our moral and political values, it has been difficult to escape the naturalistic fallacy that the key to our sex lies somewhere in the recesses of 'Nature', and that sexual science provides the best means of access to it. Not surprisingly, sexual theorists, as Murray Davis has noted, have become custodians of intellectual life, carrying out duties of guardianship and sanitation, tidying up the world by sweeping messy things into neat pigeonholes (Davis 1983: 272, note 1). Unfortunately, the 'mess' keeps returning with the wind, endlessly confusing our gaze.

Against the certainties of this tradition I intend in this essay to offer an alternative way of understanding sexuality (indeed, 'sexualities'). This involves seeing sexuality not as a primordially 'natural' phenomenon but rather as a product of social and historical forces. 'Sexuality', I shall argue, is a 'fictional unity', that once did not exist, and at some time in the future may not exist again. It is an invention of the human mind. As Carole S. Vance has suggested, 'the most important organ in humans is located between the ears' (Vance 1984).

This does not mean we can simply ignore the massive edifice of sexuality which envelops us. It has been argued that 'sexuality is without the importance ascribed to it in our contemporary society . . . it does not exist as such, because there is no such thing as sexuality' (Heath 1982: 3). Here we see a reduction to absurdity of a valuable insight. Of course sexuality exists as a palpable social presence, shaping our personal and public lives. But I am suggesting that what we define as 'sexuality' is an historical construction, which brings together a host of different biological and mental possibilities, and cultural forms – gender identity, bodily differences, reproductive capacities, needs, desires, fantasies, erotic practices, institutions and values – which need not be linked together, and in other cultures have not been. All the constituent elements of sexuality have their source either in the body or the mind, and I am not attempting to deny the limits posed by biology or mental processes. But the capacities of the body and the psyche are given meaning only in social relations. The next chapter, on 'The invention of sexuality' will attempt to justify this argument, while Chapters 3 and 4 will look at the implications of this approach for thinking about gender and sexual identities, and the fact of sexual diversity.

These chapters amount to a critique of what is now generally called the 'essentialist' approach to sex: that is a method which attempts to explain the properties of a complex whole by reference to a supposed inner truth or essence, the assumption 'that in all sexological matters there must be a single, basic, uniform pattern ordained by nature itself' (Singer 1973: 15). This is, in the language of modern critical science, a *reductionist* method in that it reduces the complexity of the world to the imagined simplicities of its constituent units; and it is *deterministic* in that it seeks to explain individuals as automatic products of inner propulsions, whether of the genes, the instinct, the hormones, or the mysterious workings of the dynamic unconscious.

Against such an approach I shall argue that the meanings we give to 'sexuality' are socially organized, sustained by a variety of languages, which seek to tell us what sex is, what it ought to be – and what it could be. Existing languages of sex, embedded in moral treatises, laws, educational practices, psychological theories, medical definitions, social rituals, pornographic or romantic fictions, popular music, as well as in commonsense assumptions (most of which disagree) set the horizon of the possible. They all present themselves up as true representations of our intimate needs and desires. The difficulty lies in their contradictory appeals, in the babel of voices they bring forth. In order to make sense of them, and perhaps to go beyond the current limits on the possible, we need to learn to translate these languages – and to develop new ones. This has been one of the tasks of those who have sought, in recent years, to 'deconstruct' the apparent unity of this world of sexuality. Together they have provided the elements of a non-essentialist concept of 'sexuality'.

From social anthropology, sociology and post-Kinsey sex research there has come a growing awareness of the vast range of sexualities that exist in other cultures and within our own culture. Other cultures, Ruth Benedict noted, act as laboratories 'in which we may study the diversity of human institutions' (Benedict 1980: 12). An awareness that the way we do things is not the only way of living can provide a salutary jolt to our ethnocentricity. It can also force us to ask questions about why things are as they are today. Other cultures, and subcultures, are a mirror to our own transitoriness. Names of writers such as the anthropologists Malinowski or Mead, the biologist Kinsey or the social psychologists and sociologists Gagnon and Simon and Plummer recur in these pages because they tell us that variety not uniformity is the norm. At the same time, the new theorists of globalization have made us aware that the new energies unleashed on the world are producing unpredictable patterns as the global and the local, the 'glocal', intermesh, clash, and engender new possibilities [2].

The legacy of Freud and his theory of the dynamic unconscious is another major source of the new sexual theory. From the tradition of psychoanalysis that he initiated has emerged a recognition that what goes on in the unconscious mind often contradicts the apparent certainties of conscious life. The life of the mind – of fantasies above all – reveals a diversity of desires to which the human being is heir. It unsettles the apparent solidities of gender, of sexual need, of identity. As Rosalind Coward has graphically said, 'In the private life of the mind, nothing is certain, nothing is fixed' (Coward 1984: 204).

Alongside these developments, the 'new social history' of recent years, with its emphasis on the history of populations and of 'mentalities', the experiences and beliefs of the downtrodden and oppressed as much as the powerful, has posed new questions about what we mean by 'the present' as well as about the 'history of the past'. *The History of Sexuality* by Michel Foucault has had a spectacular influence on modern thinking about sex because it grew out of, as well as contributed to, this fertile development of our historical understanding. Foucault, like Freud two generations earlier, stands at a crossroads of sexual thought, important as much for the questions he raises as for the answers he provides.

Finally, and most powerfully of all, the emergence of new social movements concerned with sex – modern feminism, the gay and lesbian and other radical sexual movements – have challenged many of the certainties of the 'sexual tradition', and as a result have produced new insights into the intricate forms of power and domination that shape our sexual lives. The politics of homosexuality have placed on the agenda questions about sexual preference, identity, and choice, and the arbitrariness of sexual categorizations. The women's movement has forced a recognition of the multiple forms of female sexual subordination, from endemic male violence and misogyny to sexual harassment and a pervasive language of sexual denigration and abuse. It has dramatized the institutionalized nature of 'compulsory heterosexuality'. It has demanded a recognition of women's rights over their own bodies by re-posing questions about consent and reproductive rights, desire and pleasure. Again there are as many questions posed as answers given. Differences have emerged between men and women, men and men, women and women, homosexuals and heterosexuals, black and white. No universally acceptable codes of appropriate behaviour have been elaborated despite all the heated debates. But something much more valuable has happened. We are being forced to rethink what we understand by sexuality because of a growing awareness of the tangled web of influences and forces – politics, economics, race, ethnicity, geography and space, gender, morals and values – that shape our emotions, needs, desires and relationships.

So what does a non-essentialist theory of sexuality mean for the politics of sexuality and for sexual ethics? These are the topics I examine in Chapters 5 and 6. They pose perhaps the most difficult challenges of all. The 'sexual tradition' assumed that your sex was your fate or destiny: what you desired was what you were. Sexuality pinned you down like a butterfly to the table. If you break with this tradition, if you reject the idea that sexuality embodies its own values and goals, then you are faced with complex problems of alignment and choice. Confronted by such uncertainties, it is all too easy to retreat into moral or political absolutes, to reassert again, against all the odds, against all the evidence, that there is a true sexuality that we must find at all costs. The aim of this essay is to challenge such absolutes without falling into the trap of saying no values are possible, 'anything goes'. 'Sexuality' is a deeply problematic concept, and there are no easy answers to the challenges it poses. But if we begin to ask the correct questions then we might find the way through the maze. We shall not find at the end of the journey a prescription for correct behaviour. But we might find a framework which allows us to come to terms with diversity – and to re-find, in sexuality, new opportunities for creative relationships, agency and choice.

2

THE INVENTION OF SEXUALITY

> . . . sexuality may be thought about, experienced, and acted on differ-
> ently according to age, class, ethnicity, physical ability, sexual orientation
> and preference, religion, and region.
>
> Carole S. Vance (1984: 17)

A BRIEF HISTORY OF THE HISTORY OF SEXUALITY

When I first began writing about the history of sexuality I was fond
of using a phrase from the American historian, Vern Bullough: that sex
in history was a 'virgin field' [1]. This may have been a dubious pun
but it was useful in underlining an important, if often overlooked, reality.
'Sexuality' was much talked about and written about but our historical knowledge about it remained pretty negligible. Those would-be
colonizers who ventured into the field tended either to offer transcultural
generalizations ('the history of a long warfare between the dangerous
and powerful drives and the systems of taboos and inhibitions which
man has erected to control them', Rattray Taylor 1953: 13); or to
subsume the subject under more neutral and acceptable labels ('marriage'
and 'morals' especially). Sexuality seemed marginal to the broad acres of
orthodox history.

Over the past few decades, however, much has changed, sometimes dramatically. There has been a major explosion of historical writings about sex. We now know a great deal about such topics as marriage and the family, prostitution and homosexuality, the forms of legal and medical regulation, pre-Christian and non-Christian moral codes, women's bodies and health, illegitimacy and birth control, rape and sexual violence, the evolution of sexual identities, and the importance of social networks and oppositional sexualities. Historians have deployed sophisticated methods of family reconstitution and demographic history, have intensively searched for new, or interrogated old, documentary sources, and made fuller use of oral history interviews to reconstruct the subjective or the tabooed experience. Encouraged by a vigorous grass-roots history, fed by the impact of modern feminism and gay and lesbian politics, and made urgent by the impact of the HIV/AIDS crisis which required better knowledge of human sexual behaviours, there is now an impressive library of articles, pamphlets and books. Sex research, the sociologist Ken Plummer once noted, makes you 'morally suspect' (Plummer 1975: 4). But the history of sexuality is now in danger of becoming a respectable field of study, with a high degree of professional recognition, its own specialist journals, and an interested, even passionate, audience. Writing about sexuality no longer seems quite such a bizarre and marginal activity as it once did. There is even a dawning recognition that the history of sexuality tells us more than the where's, how's and why's of the erotic: it just might throw light on our confusing and confused present, in all its complexity.

But having said this, we are still left with a dilemma – as to what exactly our object of study is. I can list, as I did above, a number of activities that we conventionally designate as sexual; but what is it that connects them? What is the magic element that defines some things as sexual and others not? There are no straightforward answers to these questions. At the heart of our concern, clearly, is an interest in the relations between men and women. One particular form of their interaction is the process of biological and social reproduction. No historian of sexuality would dare to ignore that. But a history of reproduction is not a history of sex. As Alfred Kinsey bitingly observed:

> Biologists and psychologists who have accepted the doctrine that the only natural function of sex is reproduction have simply ignored

the existence of sexual activity which is not reproductive. They have assumed that heterosexual responses are a part of an animal's innate, 'instinctive' equipment, and that all other types of sexual activity represent 'perversions' of the 'normal instincts'. Such interpretations are, however, mystical.

(Kinsey *et al.* 1953: 448)

Most erotic interactions, even between those we easily call 'heterosexual', do not lead to procreation. And there are many forms of non-heterosexual sex, amongst women, and amongst men. Some of these patterns involve intercourse of one sort or another. Others do not. Most have at least the potentiality of leading to orgasm. Yet some activities which are clearly sex-related (for example cross-dressing or transgenderism) may lead only to chance 'sexual release', or none at all. Not even intimacy seems a clear enough criterion for judging what is sexual. Some activities we quite properly describe as sexual (masturbation is a good example) do not, on the surface at least, involve any other person at all. Some aspects of intimacy have nothing to do with sex; and some sex is not intimate. In the age of cybersex, mediated anonymously through millions of network connections, bodily intimacy is in danger of being displaced altogether. Modern sociobiologists or evolutionary psychologists who wish to explain every manifestation of social life by reference to the 'timeless energy of the selfish genes', or the mating games of our remote ancestors on the African savannah half a million years ago, may see some biological logic in all of these activities. The rest of us, wisely in my opinion, are probably a little more sceptical. We are rather more than the 'survival machines – robots blindly programmed to preserve the molecule' that the populist biologist Richard Dawkins describes [2].

So what is a history of sexuality a history of? My rather disappointing answer would be that it is a history without a proper subject; or rather as Robert Padgug has suggested, a history of a subject in constant flux [3]. It is often as much a history of *our* changing preoccupations about how we should live, how we should enjoy or deny our bodies, as about the past. The way we write about our sexuality tells us as much about the present and its concerns as about this past.

We are not, of course, the first generation to speculate about the history of sexuality, nor the first to be so revealing about our preoccupations in doing so. Some sense of the past has always been an important element for those that have been thinking about the meaning and implications of erotic life. In her book *Patriarchal Precedents,* Rosalind Coward has described the complex and heated debates in the last half of the nineteenth century about the nature of contemporary family and sexual forms (Coward 1983). Pioneering social scientists saw in sexuality a privileged site for speculations on the very origins of human society. From this flowed conflicting theories about the evolution and development of the various patterns of sexual life. Had the modern family evolved from the primitive clan, or was it already there, 'naturally', at the birth of history? Did our ancestors live in a state of primitive promiscuity, or was monogamy a biological necessity and fact? Was there once an Eden of sexual egalitarianism before the 'world historical defeat of the female sex', or was patriarchal domination present from the dawn of culture? On the resolution of such debates depended attitudes not only to existing social forms (marriage, sexual inequality, the double standard of morality) but also to other, 'primitive' cultures that existed contemporaneously with the Western in other (often colonized) parts of the world. Could we find clues to our own evolutionary history in the rites and behaviours of the aborigines, apparently stunted on the ladder of progress? Or did these people tell us something else about the variability of cultures?

We have still not fully escaped the effects of these evolutionist controversies. For much of the twentieth century racist practices were legitimized by reference to the primitive condition of other races – a position hallowed, no doubt unintentionally, by the founding father of evolutionary biology himself. In the last paragraphs of his *The Descent of Man* (1871), Charles Darwin commented on the blood of more primitive creatures flowing through the native peoples he had met on his early investigatory voyages. Even those who extolled the virtues of the sexual freedom of non-industrial societies fell back on a belief that their peoples were somehow 'closer to nature', free of the stifling conventions of complex modern society. Similarly, many of the feminist debates of the 1970s and 1980s about the permanence of patriarchal male domination recultivated the ground so feverishly worked over a century previously. Yet from the 1920s the older questions about the evolution of human culture were being displaced by a new anthropological approach, which asked different questions about sexuality.

This was associated in the first place with writers such as Bronislaw Malinowski and Margaret Mead. They recognized the danger of trying to understand our own pre-history by looking at existing societies. As a result, there was a new effort to try to understand each particular society in its own terms. This gave rise to a kind of cultural relativism in looking at other sexual mores, and a recognition of the validity of different sexual systems, however exotic they may have looked by the standards of twentieth-century industrial societies. This new approach was highly influential in helping to put Western culture, with all its discontents, into some sort of context. Moreover, by recognizing the diversity of sexual patterns all over the world, it contributed to a more sympathetic understanding of the diversity of sexual patterns and cultures within our own society. Social anthropology helped to provide a critical standard by which we could begin to judge the historical nature of our own norms and values. The most famous example of this genre, Margaret Mead's romantic (and now much criticized) picture of 'coming of age' in Samoa, was enormously influential in the 1930s in large part because it seemed to demonstrate that the (repressive) American way of dealing with the problem of adolescence was neither desirable, inevitable, nor necessary [4].

There were, however, difficulties. On the one hand, there was the danger of attempting to understand all sexual acts by their function, as finely tuned responses to the claims of society. For Malinowski a grasp of the laws of society needed to be matched by a scientific understanding of the laws of nature, and he paid homage to the sexological work of Havelock Ellis, and gave critical respect to Freud for helping him to grasp 'the universally human and fundamental' [5]. Malinowski saw cultures as delicate mechanisms designed to satisfy a basic human nature; in the process, the status of 'the natural' was not so much questioned as reaffirmed, though now it was less a product of evolution and more of basic instinctual needs. On the other hand, the endorsement of an 'infinite plasticity' of human needs by Ruth Benedict, Margaret Mead and their followers led not to a more historical account of sexual patterns but to a purely descriptive anthropology in which readers were offered wonderful, shimmering evocations of the sexual lives of other peoples, but little sense of why these patterns were as they were. In the absence of any theory of determinative structures or of historical processes, again essentialist assumptions surreptitiously reasserted themselves.

The originality of contemporary attempts to develop a historical approach to sexuality lies in their willingness to question the naturalness and inevitability of the sexual categories and assumptions we have inherited. The sociologists/social psychologists Gagnon and Simon have talked of the need which may have existed at some unspecified time in the past to *invent* an importance for sexuality – perhaps because of underpopulation and threats of cultural submergence (Gagnon and Simon 1973). The French philosopher Michel Foucault has gone further by attempting to query the very category of 'sexuality' itself:

> Sexuality must not be thought of as a kind of natural given which power tries to hold in check, or as an obscure domain which knowledge tries gradually to uncover. It is the name that can be given to a historical construct.
>
> (Foucault 1979: 105)

Foucault's work has made a vital contribution to recent discussions on the history of sexuality precisely because it burst onto and grew out of work that was creatively developing in sociology, anthropology, and in radical social history. It helped to give a focus for questions already being formed. To questions about what shaped sexual beliefs and behaviours, a new one was added, concerning the history of the idea of sexuality itself. For Foucault, sexuality was a relationship of elements and discourses, a series of meaning-giving practices and activities, a social apparatus which had a history – with complex roots in the pre-Christian and Christian past, but achieving a modern conceptual unity, with diverse effects, only within the modern world.

The most important result of this historical approach to sexuality is that it opens the whole field to critical analysis and assessment. It becomes possible to relate sexuality to other social phenomena. Three types of question then become critically important. First: how is sexuality shaped, how is it articulated with economic, social and political structures, in a phrase, how is it 'socially constructed'? Second: how and why has the domain of sexuality achieved such a critical organizing and symbolic significance in Western culture; why do we think it is so important? Third: what is the relationship between sex and power; what role should we assign class divisions, patterns of male domination and racism? Coursing through each of these questions is a recurrent preoccupation: if sexuality is constructed by human agency, to what extent can it be changed? This is the question I shall attempt to deal with in succeeding chapters. The first three I shall examine in turn in the rest of this chapter.

THE 'SOCIAL CONSTRUCTION' OF SEXUALITY

The commonly used term 'the social construction of sexuality' has a harsh and mechanistic sound. But at its heart is a quite straightforward concern, with 'the intricate and multiple ways in which our emotions, desires and relationships are shaped by the society we live in' [6]. It is basically about the ways in which sexualities have been shaped in a complex history, and in tracing how sexual patterns have changed over time. It is concerned with the historical and social organization of the erotic.

In practice, most writers on our sexual past have assumed that sex is an irresistible natural energy barely held in check by a thin crust of civilization. For Malinowski:

Sex is a most powerful instinct . . . there is no doubt that masculine jealousy, sexual modesty, female coyness, the mechanism of sexual attraction and of courtship – all these forces and conditions made it necessary that even in the most primitive human aggregates there should exist powerful means of regulating, suppressing and directing this instinct.

(Malinowski 1963: 120)

'Sex', as he put it in another paper, 'really is dangerous', the source of most human trouble from Adam and Eve onwards (Malinowski 1963: 127).

In these words we can still hear echoes of Richard von Krafft-Ebing's view at the end of the nineteenth century of sex as an all-powerful instinct which demands fulfilment against the claims of morals, belief and social restrictions. But even more orthodox academic historians speak in rather similar language. Lawrence Stone, for instance, in *The Family, Sex and Marriage* sensibly rejects the idea that 'the id' (the energy of the Freudian unconscious) is the most powerful and unchanging of all drives. He suggests that changes in protein, in diet, in physical exertion and in psychic stress all have an effect on the organization of sex. Yet he still speaks of 'the super ego' (our internalized system of values) at times repressing and at other times releasing the sexual drive, which eloquently reproduces the ancient traditional picture of sexuality as a pool of energy that has to be contained or let go (Stone 1977: 15).

These approaches assume that sex offers a basic 'biological mandate' which presses against and must be restrained by the cultural matrix. This is what I mean by an essentialist approach to sexuality. It takes many forms. Liberatory theorists such as Wilhelm Reich and Herbert Marcuse tended to see sex as a beneficient force which was repressed by a corrupt civilization. Sociobiologists or contemporary evolutionary psychologists on the other hand see all social forms as in some unspecified way emanations of basic genetic material. Yet they all argue for a world of nature which provides the raw material we must use for the understanding of the social. Against all these arguments I want to stress that sexuality is shaped by social forces. And far from being the most natural element in social life, the most resistant to cultural moulding, it is perhaps one of the most susceptible to organization. Indeed I would go so far as to say that sexuality only exists through its social forms and social organization. Moreover, the forces that shape and mould the erotic possibilities of the body vary from society to society. 'Sexual socialization', Ellen Ross and Rayner Rapp have written, 'is no less specific to each culture than is socialization to ritual, dress or cuisine' (Ross and Rapp 1984: 109). This puts the emphasis firmly where it should belong, on society and social relations rather than on nature.

I do not wish to deny the importance of biology. The physiology and morphology of the body provides the preconditions for human sexuality. Biology conditions and limits what is possible. But it does not cause the patterns of sexual life. We cannot reduce human behaviour to the mysterious workings of the DNA, the eternal gene, or 'the dance of the chromosomes' (Cherfas and Gribbin 1984). I prefer to see in biology a set of potentialities, which are transformed and given meaning only in social relationships. Human consciousness and human history are very complex phenomena.

This theoretical stance has many roots: in the sociology and anthropology of sex, in the revolution in psychoanalysis and in the new social history. But despite these disparate starting points, it coheres around a number of common assumptions. First, there is a general rejection of sex as an autonomous realm, a natural domain with specific effects, a rebellious energy that the social controls. We can no longer set 'sex' against 'society' as if they were separate domains. Secondly, there is a widespread recognition of the social variability of sexual forms, beliefs, ideologies, identities and behaviour, and of the existence of different sexual cultures. Sexuality has a history, or more realistically, many histories, each of which needs to be understood both in its uniqueness and as part of an intricate pattern. Thirdly, we must abandon the idea that we can fruitfully understand the history of sexuality in terms of a dichotomy of pressure and release, repression and liberation. Sexuality is not a head of steam that must be capped lest it destroy us; nor is it a life force we must release to save our civilization. Instead we must learn to see that sexuality is something which society produces in complex ways. It is a result of diverse social practices that give meaning to human activities, of social definitions and self-definitions, of struggles between those who have power to define and regulate, and those who resist. Sexuality is not a given, it is a product of negotiation, struggle and human agency.

Nothing is sexual, Plummer has suggested, but naming makes it so (Plummer 1975). If this is the case it follows that we need to move gingerly in applying the dominant Western definitions to other cultures. Both the significance attributed to sexuality and attitudes to the various manifestations of erotic life vary enormously. Some societies display so little interest in erotic activity that they have been labelled more or less 'asexual' (Messenger 1971). Others use the erotic to open up sharp dichotomies, between those who can be included in the community of believers, and those who must be forcibly excluded; between those open to salvation, and the sinners who are not. Islamic cultures have, it is claimed, developed a lyrical view of sex with sustained attempts at integrating the religious and the sexual. Bouhdiba writes of 'the radical legitimacy of the practice of sexuality' in the Islamic world – as long, that is, as it was not homosexual, 'violently condemned' by Islam, or involved extra-marital activity by women, who might be condemned to death under Sharia law (Bouhdiba 1985: 159, 200). The Christian West, notoriously, has seen in sex a terrain of moral anguish and conflict, setting up an enduring dualism between the spirit and the flesh, the mind and the body. It has had the inevitable result of creating a cultural configuration which simultaneously disavows the body while being obsessively preoccupied with it.

Within the wide parameters of general cultural attitudes, each culture labels different practices as appropriate or inappropriate, moral or immoral, healthy or perverted. Western culture, at least as codified by the Roman Catholic and evangelical traditions, continues formally at least to define appropriate behaviour in terms of a limited range of acceptable activities. Monogamous marriage between partners of roughly equal age but different genders remains the most widely accepted norm (though not, of course, necessarily or even today generally the reality) and, despite many changes, the most readily accepted gateway to adulthood, and sexual activity. Homosexuality, on the other hand, despite remarkable shifts in attitudes over recent generations, still carries in many quarters a heavy legacy of taboo. Homosexuals may be accepted today, Dennis Altman remarked in the early 1980s, but homosexuality is not, and in a climate where a health crisis around HIV/AIDS easily led soon afterwards to a moral panic about gay lifestyles, this rang true [7]. Much has changed, even since the 1980s, but traditional homophobic norms and values remain deeply embedded.

Other cultures, on the other hand, have not found it necessary to issue the same injunctions, or develop the same dichotomies. The anthropologists Ford and Beach found that only 15 per cent of 185 different societies surveyed restricted sexual liaisons to single mateships. Kinsey's figures suggested that beneath a surface conformity Western practices are as varied: in his 1940s sample, 50 per cent of males and 26 per cent of females had extra-marital sex by the age of 40 [8]. Even more unsettling was the evidence that the heterosexual/ homosexual binary divide, which has done so much to define Western attitudes since the nineteenth century, was something less than universal.

Marriage has not been inevitably heterosexual, even before contemporary claims for the recognition of same-sex partnerships. Amongst the Nuer, older women 'marry' younger women; and there is a great deal of emerging evidence that even in early Christian Europe male partnerships were sanctified by the Church almost as if they were marriages (Edholm 1982; Boswell 1994). Homosexuality has not been universally tabooed. There have been various forms of institutionalized homosexuality, from puberty rites in various tribal societies, to pedagogic relations between older men and youths (as in Ancient Greece), to the integrated transvestite partnerships (the berdache) among native Americans, and transgendered identities amongst other peoples, from

Brazil to the Philippines (Herdt 1994; Parker 1991, 1999; Parker *et al.* 2000).

Many in the West, not least in the formal positions of the Roman Catholic Church, still tend to define the norms of sex in relationship to one of the possible results – reproduction. For long centuries of Christian dominance it was *the only* justification of sexual relations. Other cultures, however, have sometimes failed even to make the connection between copulation and procreation. Some societies only recognize the role of the father, others the mother. The Trobriand Islanders investigated by Malinowski saw no connection between intercourse and reproduction. It was only *after* the spirit child entered the womb that intercourse assumed any significance for them, in moulding the character of the future child (Malinowski 1929).

Sexual cultures are precisely that: culturally specific, shaped by a wide range of social factors. By definition, there can be no such thing as a culture which ignores the erotic. Each culture makes what Plummer calls 'who restrictions' and 'how restrictions'. 'Who restrictions' are concerned with the gender of the partners, the species, age, kin, race, caste or class which limit whom we may take as partners. 'How restrictions' have to do with the organs that we use, the orifices we may enter, the manner of sexual involvement and sexual intercourse: what we may touch, when we may touch, with what frequency, and so on (Plummer 1984). These regulations take many forms: formal and informal, legal and extra-legal. They tend not to apply in an undifferentiated way for the whole of society. For instance, there are usually different rules for men and women, shaped in ways which subordinate women's sexuality to men's. There are different rules for adults and children. These rules are often more acceptable as abstract norms than as practical guides. But they provide the permissions, prohibitions, limits and possibilities through which erotic life is constructed.

Five broad areas stand out as being particularly crucial in the social organization of sexuality: kinship and family systems, economic and social organization, social regulation, political interventions, and the development of 'cultures of resistance'.

(1) Kinship and family systems

Kinship and family systems *appear* as the most basic and unchanging forms of all – pre-eminently the 'natural' focus of sexual socialization and experience. The taboo on incest, that is the prohibition of sexual involvement within certain degrees of relationship, seems to be a universal law, marking the passage, it has been often argued, from a state of nature to human society: it has been seen as constitutive of culture. (It is also the basis for our most enduring myth – that of Oedipus, who killed his father and married his mother, and then had to pay the painful price of this infringement of the Law.) Yet the forms of the taboo vary enormously. In the Christian traditions of the Middle Ages, marriage to the seventh degree of relationship was prohibited. Today, marriage to first cousins is allowed. In the Egypt of the pharoahs, sibling marriages were permitted, and in some cases so were father–daughter marriages, in the interests of preserving the purity of the royal line (Renvoize 1982). Today, father–daughter incest is amongst the most tabooed of activities. The existence of the incest taboo illustrates the need of all societies to regulate sex – but not how it is done. Even 'blood relationships' have to be interpreted through the grid of culture.

The truth is that kin ties are not *natural* links of blood but are social relations between groups, often based on residential affinities and hostile to genetic affinities. Marshall Sahlins has argued that:

> human conceptions of kinship may be so far from biology as to exclude all but a small fraction of a person's genealogical connections from the category of 'close kin', while at the same time, including in that category, as sharing common blood, very distantly related people or even complete strangers. Among these strangers (genetically) may be one's own children (culturally).
>
> (Sahlins 1976: 75)

Who we decide are kin and what we describe as 'the family' are clearly dependent on a range of historical factors. There are many different family forms especially within highly industrialized, Western societies – between different classes, and different geographic, religious, racial and ethnic groups. Today many people speak of 'families of choice', based on friendships networks and chosen kin. There are 'non-heterosexual families' as well as traditional families residing next to each other, more or less in harmony. Family patterns are shaped and re-shaped by economic factors, by rules of inheritance, by state interventions to regulate marriage and divorce, or to support the family by social welfare or taxation policies. All these affect the likely patterns of sexual life: by encouraging or discouraging the rate of marriage, age of marriage, incidence of repro- duction, attitudes to non-procreative or non-heterosexual sex, acceptance of cohabitation, or single parenthood, the relative power of men over women, and so on. These factors are important in themselves. They are doubly important because the family is the arena in which most people, certainly in Western cultures, gain some sense of their individual sexual needs and identities, and if we follow psychoanalysis, it is the arena where our desires are organized from a very early stage indeed. As kin and family patterns change, so will attitudes and beliefs concerning sexuality.

(2) Economic and social organization

As I have suggested, families themselves are not autonomous, natural entities. They, too, are shaped by wider social relations. Domestic patterns can be changed: by economic forces, by the class divisions to which economic change gives rise, by the degree of urbanization and of rapid industrial and social change [9]. Labour migrations have, for example, affected patterns of courtship and have helped dictate the incidence of illegitimacy rates, or the spread of sexual diseases. The proletarianization of the rural population in early nineteenth-century England helped to contribute to the massive rise of illegitimacy during this period as old courtship patterns were broken by economic and industrial dislocation – a case of 'marriage frustrated' rather than a conscious sexual revolution. Work conditions can dramatically shape sexual lives. A good example of this is provided by the evidence for the 1920s and 1930s in Britain that women who worked in factories tended to be much more familiar with methods of artificial birth control, and thus could limit their family size to a greater degree, than women who worked solely in the home or in domestic service (Gittins 1982).

The relations between men and women are constantly affected by changes in economic and social conditions. The growing involvement of married women in the paid workforce from the 1950s and 1960s in most Western countries has inevitably affected the patterns of domestic life, even if it has yet to transform beyond recognition the traditional division of labour in the household. Increasing economic opportunities for women have been important elements in the 'rise of women' since the 1960s, perhaps the most important social transformation of the twentieth century. It has gone hand in hand with greater recognition of the sexual autonomy of women.

Such changes are no longer confined to the highly industrialized heartlands of the North of the globe. The processes of globalization are sweeping away old economic, social and cultural boundaries. Many of its manifestations are not new. Mass movements of peoples, within countries, and across states and continents, have been amongst the dominant forces of the past few hundred years – through colonization, the slave trade, the disruptive effects of war, voluntary migration, and enforced resettlements. All these have disrupted traditional patterns of life, and settled sexual values and behaviours, as men and women, adults and children have been brought together and violently parted, with unpredictable results on sexual mores – from enforced segregation of the sexes to child prostitution, from the disruption of traditional patterns of courtship and marriage, to the epidemic spread of HIV/AIDS. All the evidence suggests that contemporary global trends are speeding up these processes, creating dramatic new patterns of 'global sex'. Sexuality is not *determined* by the developing modes of production, but the rhythms of economic and social life, provide the basic preconditions and ultimate limits for the organization and 'political economy' of sexual life (Altman 2001).

(3) Social regulation

If economic life establishes some of the fundamental rhythms, the actual forms of regulation of sexuality have a considerable autonomy. Formal methods of regulating sexual life vary from time to time depending on the significance of religion, the changing role of the state, the existence or not of a moral consensus which regulates marriage patterns, divorce rates and incidence of sexual unorthodoxy. One of the critical shifts of the last hundred years in most highly industrialized countries has been the move away from moral regulation by the churches to a more secular mode of organization through medicine, education, psychology, social work and welfare practices. It is also important to recognize that the effects of these interventions are not necessarily pre-ordained. As often as not sexual life is altered by the unintended consequences of social action as much as through the intention of the authors. Laws banning obscene publications more often than not give rise to court cases that publicize them. Banning sexy films gives them a fame they might not otherwise deserve. Injunctions against artificial birth control methods can make people aware of their existence. It is surely no accident that Italy, the home of the Papacy, which strictly forbids abortion and birth control, has one of the lowest birth rates in Europe, whilst still remaining formally Catholic. Though religion can still be decisive, people are increasingly willing to decide for themselves how they want to behave. Morality is being privatized. Laws and prohibitions designed to control the behaviour of certain groups of people can actually give rise to an enhanced sense of identity and cohesion amongst them. This certainly seems to be the case with the refinement of the laws relating to male homosexuality since the late nineteenth century, which coincide with the strengthening of same-sex identities (Weeks 1977).

But it is not only formal methods which shape sexuality; there are many informal and customary patterns which are equally important. The traditional forms of regulation of adolescent courtship can be critical means of social control. It is very difficult to break with the consensus of one's village or one's peer group in school, and this is as much true today as it was in the pre-industrial societies. A language of sexual abuse ('slags', 'sluts', 'whores' in familiar Anglo-Saxon usage) works to keep girls in line, and to enforce conventional distinctions between girls who do and girls who don't. Such informal methods enforced by strictly adhered to rules often produce, by contemporary standards, various bizarre manifestations of sexual behaviour. One such example is provided by the traditional form of courtship in parts of England and Wales up to the nineteenth century known as 'bundling', which involved intimate but fully clothed rituals of sex play in bed. Closer to the present, we can find the equally exotic phenomenon of 'petting', which much preoccupied moralists and parents until the 1960s. Petting is dependent on the belief that while intercourse in public is tabooed, other forms of play, because they are not defined as *the* sex act, may be intimately engaged in. Kinsey noted in the early 1950s that:

Foreign travellers are sometimes amazed at the open display of such obviously erotic activity . . . There is an increasing amount of petting which is carried on in such public conveyances as buses, trams, and airplanes. The other passengers have learned to ignore such activities if they are pursued with some discretion. Orgasm is sometimes achieved in the petting which goes on in such public places.

(Kinsey *et al.* 1953: 259)

But petting itself becomes insignificant when the taboos against sexual intercourse before marriage are relaxed, as they have been in most Western societies since the 1960s. Implicit in such phenomena are intricate though only semiconscious rules which limit what can and cannot be done. Informal methods of regulation can have important social effects – in limiting, for example, illegitimate conceptions. They have often been enforced in the past by customary patterns of public shaming, rituals of humiliation and public mocking – examples include the 'charivari' and 'rough music' in Britain, which have widespread echoes across the globe – which serve to reinforce the norms of the community.

(4) Political interventions

These formal and informal methods of control exist within a changing political framework. The balance of political forces at any particular time can determine the degree of legislative control or moral intervention in sexual life. The general social climate provides the context in which some issues take on a greater significance than others. The existence of skilled 'moral entrepreneurs' able to articulate and call up inchoate currents of opinion can be decisive in enforcing existing legislation or in conjuring up new. The success of the New Right in America during the 1970s and 1980s in establishing an agenda for sexual conservatism by campaigning against sexual liberals and/or sexual deviants under-lines the possibilities of political mobilization around sex. In particular, the anti-abortion position of many moral conservatives opened up a fundamental divide in American politics that became a central feature of the so-called 'culture wars'. But examples abound across the world of the exploitation of sexual issues to advance or consolidate a political agenda – whether President Mugabe mixing anti-colonial and anti-gay messages to shore up his crumbling base in Zimbabwe, or fundamentalist regimes asserting their purity by stoning adulterers and homosexuals (see essays in Weeks *et al.* 2003).

(5) Cultures of resistance

But the history of sexuality is not a simple history of control, it is also a history of opposition and resistance to moral codes. Forms of moral regulation give rise to transgressions, subversions and cultures of resistance. A prime example of these is provided by the female networks of knowledge about sexuality, especially birth control and abortion, which can be seen across history and cultures. As Angus McLaren has put it:

> In studying abortion beliefs it is possible to glimpse aspects of a separate female sexual culture that supports the independence and autonomy of women from medical men, moralists and spouses.
>
> (McLaren 1984: 147)

There is a long history of such alternative knowledge. A classic example is provided by the widespread use of the lead compound diachylon in the late nineteenth century and early twentieth century in the Midlands of England. Widely used as an antiseptic, it was accidentally discovered that this could be used to induce abortions and there is evidence of its subsequent spread as a prophylactic amongst working-class women up to the outbreak of the First World War (McLaren 1978: 390).

Other examples of cultural resistance come from the emergence of the subcultures and networks established by sexual minorities. There is a long history of subcultures of male homosexuality throughout the history of the West, manifest for instance in Italian towns of the late Middle Ages, and in England from the late seventeenth century. These have been critical for the emergence of modern homosexual identities, which have been largely formed in these wider social networks. More recently, over the last hundred years or so, there have been series of explicit oppositional political movements organized around sexuality and sexual issues. The classic example is that of feminism. But in addition recent historical work has demonstrated the longstanding existence of sex reform movements often closely linked to campaigns for homosexual rights: the modern gay and lesbian movements have antecedents going

*doesn't this imply a univ-
essential? erotic
sexuality-
nath the*

back to the nineteenth century in countries like Germany and Britain (Weeks 1977).

What we so confidently know as 'sexuality' is, then, a product of many influences and social interventions. It does not exist outside history but is a historical product. This is what we mean by historical making, the cultural construction, and social organization of sexuality.

THE IMPORTANCE OF SEXUALITY

All societies have to make arrangements for the organization of erotic life. Not all, however, do it with the same obsessive concern as the West. Throughout the history of the West, since the time of the Ancient Greeks, what we call sexuality has been an object of moral concern, but the concept of sexual life has not been the same. For the Ancient Greeks concern with the pleasures of the body – *aphrodisia* – was only one, and not necessarily the most important of the preoccupations of life, to be set alongside dietary regulations and the organization of household relations. And the object of debate was quite different too. Freud, with his usual perceptiveness, was able to sum up one aspect of this difference:

> The most striking distinction between the erotic life of antiquity and our own no doubt lies in the fact that the ancients laid the stress upon the instinct itself, whereas we emphasise its object.
>
> (Freud 1905: 149)

We are preoccupied *with whom* we have sex, the ancients with the question of excess or over-indulgence, activity and passivity. Plato would have banned pederasty from his city not because it was against nature, but because it was in excess of what nature demands. Sodomy was excessively licentious, and the moral question was not whether you had sex with a man if you were a man, but whether you were active or passive. Passive homosexual activities and the people who practised them were rejected not because they were homosexual but because they involved a man acting like a woman or child. This is a distinction we can see across many cultures, where homosexual activity amongst men was tolerated as long as it did not 'feminize' the man (Veyne 1985: 27; Halperin 1990, 2002). Northern European and American societies, on the other hand, have since the nineteenth century at least been obsessively concerned whether a person is normal or abnormal, defined in terms of whether we are heterosexual or homosexual. They seek the truth of their natures in the organization of sexual desires. The differences between the two patterns represent a major shift in the organizing significance given to sexuality.

The development of the dominant Western model is the product of a long and complicated history. But there seem to be several key moments in its evolution. One came with innovations of the first century AD in the classical world, before the generalized advent of a Christianized West. It was represented by a new austerity and by a growing disapproval of *mollities,* that is, sex indulged in purely for pleasure. The Church accepted and refined the view that husbands should not behave incontinently with wives in marriage. The purpose of sex was reproduction, so sex outside marriage was obviously for pleasure and hence a sin. As Flandrin has said, 'marriage was a kind of preventive medicine given by God to save man from immorality' (Flandrin 1985: 115). The sins of the flesh were a constant temptation from the divine path.

The second crucial moment came in the twelfth and thirteenth centuries, after a series of intense critical and religious struggles, with the triumph of the Christian tradition of sex and marriage. This did not necessarily affect everyone's behaviour in society. What it did do was to establish a new norm which was enforced by both the religious and the secular arm. Marriage was a matter of family arrangement for the good of families. So for two people thrown together often as strangers, a tight set of rules had to be elaborated. As a result, 'the couple were not alone in their marriage bed: the shadow of the confessor loomed over their frolics' (Flandrin 1985: 115). Theologians and canonists discussed the sex lives of married couples to the last detail, not simply as an intellectual game but to provide detailed answers to practical moral questions.

The third crucial, and decisive, moment occurred in the eighteenth and nineteenth centuries with the increasing definition of sexual normality in terms of relations with the opposite sex, and the consequent categorization of other forms as deviant (Laqueur 1990). This last change is the one of which we are immediate heirs. It was represented by a shift from religious organization of moral life to increasingly secular regulation embodied in the emergence of new medical, psychological and educational norms. Alongside this, new typologies of degeneracy and perversion emerged and there was a decisive growth of new sexual identities. Homosexuality moved from being a category of sin to become a psychosocial disposition. Sexology began to speculate about the laws of sex and 'sexuality' finally emerged as a separate continent of knowledge with its own distinct effects.

The emergence of the category of homosexuality and 'the homosexual' illustrates what was taking place. Homosexual activities are of course widespread in all cultures and there is a sustained history of homosexuality in the West. But the idea that there is such a thing as *the* homosexual person is a relatively new one. All the evidence suggests that before the eighteenth century homosexuality, interpreted in its broadest sense as involving erotic activities between people of the same gender, certainly existed, but 'homosexuals' in any meaningful modern sense, did not. Certain acts such as sodomy were severely condemned: in Britain they carried the death penalty, formally at least, until 1861, but there seems to have been little idea of a distinct type of homosexual personage. The 'sodomite' cannot be seen as equivalent to 'homosexual'. Sodomy was not a specifically homosexual crime; the law applied indifferently to relations between men and women, men and beasts, as well as men and men. And while by the eighteenth century the persistent sodomite was clearly perceived as a special type of person, he was still defined by the nature of his act rather than the character of his personality. From the early eighteenth century, however, historians have traced the evolution of new sexual types, third and even fourth sexes. From the mid-nineteenth century 'the homosexual' (the term 'homosexuality' was invented in the 1860s) was increasingly seen as belonging to a particular species of being, characterized by feelings, latency and a psychosexual condition. This view was elaborated by pioneering sexologists who produced ever more complex explanations and descriptions. Was homosexuality a product of corruption or degeneration, congenital or the result of childhood trauma? Was it a natural variation or a perverse deformation? Should it be tolerated or subjected to cure? Havelock Ellis distinguished the invert from the pervert, Freud the 'absolute invert', the 'amphigenic' and the 'contingent'. Rather later, Clifford Allen distinguished twelve types, ranging from the compulsive, the nervous, the neurotic and the psychotic to the psychopathic and the alcoholic. Kinsey invented a seven-point rating for the spectrum of heterosexual/

homosexual behaviour, which allowed his successors to distinguish a 'Kinsey one' from a 'five' or 'six' as if real life depended upon it [10].

This labelling and pigeonholing energy and zeal has led a number of historians to argue that the emergence of distinct categories of sexual beings over the past century is the consequence of a sustained effort at social control. Writers on the history of lesbianism have suggested that the development of a sexualized lesbian identity at the end of the nineteenth century and early twentieth century was an imposition by sexologists designed precisely to split women from women, breaking the ties of emotionality and affection which bind all women together against men (Faderman 1981). There is clearly an element of truth in this. Nevertheless I think it much more credible to see the emergence of distinct identities during this period as the product of struggle against prevailing norms, which had necessarily different effects for men and women. Sexologists did not so much invent the homosexual or the lesbian as attempt to put into their own characteristic pathologizing language changes that were taking place before their eyes. Pioneering sexologists like Krafft-Ebing were confronted by people appearing in the courts or coming to them for help, largely as a result of a new politically motivated zeal to control more tightly aberrant manifestations of sexual desire. The definition of homosexuality as a distinct form of sexual desire was one attempt to come to terms with this new reality. Krafft-Ebing found himself in an unlikely alliance with articulate defenders of their own sexualities, to explain and even justify it. This in turn produced an inevitable response in the urge to self-definition, and the articulation of new sexual identities (Oosterhuis 2000).

Sexual activity was increasingly coming to define a particular type of person. In return people were beginning to define themselves as different, and their difference was constituted around their sexuality. One Thomas Newton was arrested in London in 1726, entrapped by a police informant in a homosexual act. Confronted by the police he said: 'I did it because I thought I knew him, and I think there is no crime in making what use I please of my own body' (Bray 1982: 114). Here we can see, embryonically, the urge to self-definition that was to flourish in the proliferation of homosexual identities in the twentieth century. In turn, the growth of the category of the homosexual at the end of the nineteenth century presaged a profusion of new sexual types and identities in the twentieth century: the transvestite, the transsexual, the bisexual, the paedophile, the sado-masochist and so on. Increasingly in the twentieth century people defined themselves by defining their sex. The question we have to ask is why sexuality has become so central to our definition of self and of normality.

Sexuality, it can be argued, is shaped at the juncture of two major axes of concern: with our subjectivity – who and what we are; and with society – with the future growth, well-being, health and prosperity of the population as a whole. The two are intimately connected because at the heart of both is the body and its potentialities. 'As the human body becomes autonomous and self-conscious', Lowe has written, that is, as it becomes the object of a fully secular attention:

> as emotion recoiled from the world and became more cooped up, sexuality in bourgeois society emerged as an explicit phenomenon.
>
> (Lowe 1982: 100)

And as society has become more and more concerned with the lives of its members, for the sake of moral uniformity, economic well-being, national security or hygiene and health, so it has become more and more preoccupied with the sex lives of its individuals, giving rise to intricate methods of administration and management, to a flowering of moral anxieties, medical, hygienic, legal and welfarist interventions, or scientific delving, all designed to understand the self by understanding sex.

Sexuality as a result has become an increasingly important social and political as well as moral issue. If we look at all the major crises in Britain since the beginning of the nineteenth century (and this can be echoed in all the major industrializing and urbanizing societies, other things being equal) we see that in one way or another a preoccupation with sex has been integral to them. In the crisis of the French revolutionary wars in the early nineteenth century one of the central preoccupations of ideologists was with the moral decline which it was believed had set off the train of events leading to the collapse of the French monarchy. In the 1830s and 1840s, with the first crisis of the new industrial society, there was an obsessive concern with the sexuality of women and the threat to children who worked in the factories and mines. By the mid-nineteenth century, attempts to re-order society focused on the question of moral hygiene and health. From the 1860s to the 1890s prostitution, the moral standards of society and moral reform were at the heart of public debate, many seeing in moral decay a sign of impending imperial decline. In the early decades of the twentieth century these concerns were re-ordered in a new concern with the quality of the British population. The vogue for eugenics, the planned breeding of the best in society, though never dominant, had a significant influence in shaping both welfare policies and the attempt to re-order national priorities in the face of international competition. Inevitably it fed into a burgeoning racism during the first half of the twentieth century. During the inter-war years and into the 1940s, the decline of the birthrate engendered fevered debates about the merits of birth control, selective encouragement of family planning policies, and the country falling into the hands of the once subject races. By the 1950s, in the period of the Cold War, there was a new searching out of sexual degenerates, especially homosexuals, because they were apparently curiously susceptible to treachery. This was to become a major aspect of the McCarthyite witch hunt in the USA which had echoes in Britain and elsewhere. By the 1980s in the wake of several decades of so-called permissiveness, minority forms of sexuality, especially homosexuality, were being blamed for the decline of the family, and for the return of epidemics (in the form of AIDS), and a new moral conservatism gave new energy to a revival of right-wing political forces. Yet by the turn of the new Millennium, whilst moral fundamentalism still flourished across the globe, it had become clear that rapid social and cultural change were relentlessly undermining traditional patterns, giving rise to a heightened sexual individualism, and new claims for 'sexual citizenship'. In many Western countries, particularly, sexuality had reached the heart of the political agenda.

A series of concerns are crystallized in all these crises and critical moments: with the norms of family life, the relations between men and women, the nature of female sexuality, the question of sexual variation, the relations between adults and children, and so on. These are critical issues in any society. The debates about them in much of the West over the last few decades have been heated precisely because debates about sexuality are debates about the nature of society: as sex goes, so goes society; as society goes, so goes sexuality.

SEXUALITY AND POWER

This is another way of saying that issues of sexuality are increasingly important in the whole working of power in contemporary society. I mentioned earlier that one of the effects of a historical approach to sexuality was to see power over sexuality as productive rather than negative or repressive. The metaphor of repression comes from hydraulics: it offers the image of a gushing energy that must be held in check. The historical approach to sexuality would stress rather the impact of various social practices and discourses that construct sexual regulations, give meaning to bodily activities, shape definitions and limit and control human behaviour.

The rejection of a repression model (what Foucault called the 'repressive hypothesis') does not of course mean that all regimes of sexual regulation are of equal force or effectiveness. Some are clearly more harsh, authoritarian and oppressive than others. One of the important results of the new historical investigation of sexuality has been a reassessment of the whole Victorian period. Classically this has been seen as a period of unique moral hypocrisy and sexual denial. It is now increasingly apparent that this is highly misleading. Far from witnessing an avoidance of sex, the nineteenth century was not far from being obsessed with sexual issues. Rather than being the subject that was hidden away, it was a topic that was increasingly discussed in relation to diverse aspects of social life. This does not mean, however, that the Victorian period can now be seen as peculiarly liberal. In England the death penalty for sodomy was still on the statute book until 1861. Restrictions on female sexual autonomy were severe and the distinction between respectable women and the unregenerates (the virgin and the whore, the madonna and the magdalen) reached their apogee during this period. Although the present may not have produced a perfect resolution of all conflict, for many of us it is infinitely preferable to what existed little more than a hundred years ago.

The usefulness of abandoning the repressive model, in its crude form, however, is that it does direct us towards an attempt to understand the actual mechanisms of power at work in any particular period. Power no longer appears a single entity which is held or controlled by a particular group, gender, state or ruling class. It is, in Schur's phrase, 'more like a process than an object' (Schur 1980: 7), a malleable and mobile force which takes many different forms and is exercised through a variety of different social practices and relationships. If this approach to power is adopted then we need to abandon any theoretical approach which sees sexuality moulded by a dominant, determining will – whether it be of 'society', as functionalist sociology tended to suggest, or 'capitalism', as Marxists might argue, or 'patriarchy' or 'men', as some feminists would propose. Power does not operate through single mechanisms of control. It operates through complex and overlapping – and often contradictory – mechanisms, which produce domination *and* oppositions, subordination *and* resistances.

There are many structures of domination and subordination in the world of sexuality but three major axes seem peculiarly important today: those of class, of gender, and of race.

(1) Class

Class differences in sexual regulation are not unique to the modern world. In the slave-owning society of pre-Christian Rome, moral standards varied with social status. 'To be *impudicus* (that is passive) is disgraceful for a free man', wrote the elder Seneca, 'but it is the slave's absolute obligation towards his master, and the freed man owes a moral duty of compliance' (Veyne 1985: 31). What was true in the ancient world has become more sharply apparent in the modern. It has in fact been argued (by Foucault) that the very idea of 'sexuality' is an essentially bourgeois one, which developed as an aspect of the self-definition of a class, both against the decadent aristocracy and the rampant 'immorality' of the lower orders in the course of the eighteenth and nineteenth centuries. It was a colonizing system of beliefs which sought to remould the polity in its own image. The respectable standards of family and domestic life, with the increased demarcations between male and female roles, a growing ideological distinction between private and public life, and a marked concern with moral and hygienic policing of non-marital, non-heterosexual sexuality, was increasingly the norm by which all behaviour was judged. This does not, of course, mean that all or even most behaviour conformed to the norm. There is plentiful evidence that the behaviour of the working classes remained extremely resilient to middle-class manners, producing its own complex rules and rituals. Nevertheless, the sexual patterns that exist in the twenty-first century are a product of a social struggle in which class was a vital element. This resulted, not surprisingly, in distinct class patterns of sexual life. Kinsey's American sample of 18,000 in the 1940s suggested that whether it be on masturbation, homosexuality, the incidence of oral sex, petting, concourse with prostitutes, pre-marital or extra-marital sex, or 'total sexual outlet', there were significantly different class patterns amongst men. For women, on the other hand, class differences played a relatively minor part: their age and gender ideologies were much more critical factors in shaping behaviour. Later surveys, while taking note of the gradual erosion of class boundaries, have confirmed the continuing existence of class sexualities. It is hardly surprising, then, that the literature abounds with images of relations between men and women (and indeed between men and men, and women and women) where class, power and sexual desire are intricately interwoven.

(2) Gender

Class, as we have seen, is not an undifferentiated category. Classes consist of men and women, and class and status differences may not have the same significance for women as for men. Gender is a crucial divide.

A number of feminist writers have seen the elaboration of sexual difference as crucial to the oppression of women, with sexuality not merely reflecting but being fundamental to the construction and maintenance of the power relations between women and men [11]. There clearly is a close relationship between the organization of gender and sexuality. Sexuality is constituted in a highly gendered world. At the same time, we cannot simply derive sexual subjectivities from gender. That would give it an *a priori* significance that would deny the intricacies in the social organization of sexuality. Nevertheless, the patterns of female sexuality are inescapably a product of the historically rooted power of men to define and categorize what is necessary and desirable. 'To be a woman', Rosalind Coward has said:

> is to be constantly addressed, to be constantly scrutinised . . . Female desire is crucial to our whole social structure. Small wonder it is so closely obscured, so endlessly pursued, so frequently recast and reformulated.
>
> (Coward 1984: 13)

And it is, of course, still pursued, recast and reformulated by men. As Richard Dyer has put it, male sexuality is a bit like air: 'you breathe it in all the time, but you aren't aware of it much' (Dyer 1985: 28). We look at the world through our concepts of male sexuality so that even when we are not looking at male sexuality as such we are looking at the world within its framework of reference.

This framework is of course the result of more than the contingencies of biology, or the inevitability of sexual difference. It is constituted by a historically specific organization of sexuality and gender. This has been variously theorized as 'compulsory heterosexuality', institutionalized heterosexuality, the 'heterosexual matrix', 'heteronormativity' – the labels reflect different theoretical positions and political positions, but they all point to a key understanding. Sexuality is in complex, but inextricable, ways locked into the structuring of gender, and both are locked together by the heterosexual assumption. The binary divides between masculinity and femininity, and between heterosexuality and homosexuality (with the first term in each couplet as the dominant one) still positions sexual subjects, and organizes sexual desire, in contemporary societies, in ways which subordinate women and marginalize the transgressor.

It would be wrong, however, to see this structuring as either monolithic or unchallenged. The law, medicine, even popular opinion is highly contradictory and changes over time. Before the eighteenth century female sexuality was regarded as voracious and all-consuming. In the nineteenth century there was a sustained effort to inform the population that female sexuality amongst respectable women just did not exist. In the later twentieth century there was a general incitement to female sexuality as an aid to all forms of consumerism. The sexuality of women has at various times been seen as dangerous, as a source of disease, as the means of transmitting national values in the age of eugenics, as the guardian of moral purity in debates over sex education, and as the main focus of attention in the debates over permissiveness and sexual liberation in the 1960s. Female sexuality has been limited by economic and social dependence, by the power of men to define sexuality, by the limitations of marriage, by the burdens of reproduction and by the endemic fact of male violence against women. At the same time, these contradictory definitions have as often provided the opportunity for women to define their own needs and desires. Since the late nineteenth century the acceptable spaces for self-definition have expanded rapidly to include not only pleasure in marriage but also relatively respectable forms of unmarried and non-procreative heterosexual activity. As Vance observes, gross and public departures from '"good" woman status' – such as lesbianism, promiscuity or non-traditional heterosexuality – still invite, and are used to justify, violation and violence (Vance 1984: 4). The patterns of male privilege have not been broken. At the same time, the real changes of the past century and the long-term impact of feminism testify that these patterns are neither inevitable nor immutable. There is plentiful evidence of 'crisis tendencies' in hegemonic masculinity, and of major, if uneven, transformations in the position of women. Each is reflected in the shifting conceptualizations of male and female sexuality.

(3) Race

Categorizations by class or gender intersect with those of ethnicity and race. Historians of sex have not actually ignored race in the past, but they have fitted it into their pre-existing framework. So the evolutionary model of sexuality put forward by the theorists of the late nineteenth century inevitably presented the non-white person – 'the savage' – as lower down the evolutionary scale than the white, as closer to nature. This view survived even in the culturally relativist and apparently liberal writings of anthropologists such as Margaret Mead. One of the attractions of her portrayal of Samoan life was precisely the idea that Samoans were in some indefinable sense freer of constraints and closer to nature than contemporary Americans. A most abiding myth is that of the insatiability of the sexual needs of non-European peoples and the threat they consequently pose for the purity of the white race. A fear of black male priapism, and the converse exploitation of black women to service their white masters, was integral to slave society in the American South in the nineteenth century and continued to shape black–white relationships well into the twentieth century. In apartheid South Africa the prohibitions of the Mixed Marriages Act and section 16 of the Immorality Act designed to prevent miscegenation were among the first pieces of apartheid legislation to be introduced after the National Party came to power on a policy of racial segregation in 1948. As the regime attempted to deal with the crisis of apartheid in the 1980s by reshaping its forms, one of the first pillars of apartheid it attempted to remove were precisely these Acts. As a result the regime came under heavy criticism from extreme right-wing groups which argued that the whole edifice of apartheid would be undermined if the laws were repealed. That of course proved to be the case. On a global scale, the belief in the superiority of European norms was perhaps most clearly revealed in the obsessive Western concern with the population explosion of the Third World, which led to various efforts on the part of development agencies as well as local authorities to impose Western patterns of artificial birth control, sometimes with disastrous results as the delicate ecology of social life was unbalanced. It should serve to remind us that modern attitudes to birth control are rooted both in women's desire to limit their own fertility and also in a eugenic and 'family planning' policy whose aim was the survival and fitness of the European races. Elements of this eugenicist past long remained in everyday practices. In Israel, Jewish families received higher child allowances than Arab ones, while in Britain the dangerous contraceptive injection, Depo Provera, was given virtually exclusively to black and very poor women. One study in the 1980s found more birth control leaflets in family planning clinics in Asian languages than in English.

Behind all such examples is a long history of the encounters between the imperial heartlands and the colonized peoples in which the latter's erotic patterns were constituted as 'other', and inferior. The process has been encoded in a series of practices, from immigration laws to birth control propaganda, from medical attitudes to the pathologizing in psychology and sociology of different patterns of family life [12]. As Stoler argues, via the colonial encounters, an 'implicit racial grammar underwrote the sexual regimes of bourgeois culture' (Stoler 1995: 9). Western notions of racial purity and sexual virtue – that is, norms of white sexuality – were in large part constituted by rejection of the colonized 'other'.

The boundaries of race, gender and class inevitably overlap. Ethnic minorities who are most subject to racist practices tend to be working class or poor, socially excluded in a variety of ways, while the definition of membership within the ethnic group can often depend on performing gender and sexual attributes successfully. Power operates subtly through a complex series of interlocking practices. As a result political challenges to oppressive forms are complex and sometimes contradictory. Sexual politics therefore can never be a single form of activity. They are enmeshed in the whole network of social contradictions and antagonisms that make up the modern world. There is, however, an important point that we can draw from this discussion. Instead of seeing sexuality as a unified whole, we have to recognize that there are various forms of sexuality: there are in fact many sexualities. There are class sexualities, and gender-specific sexualities, there are racialized sexualities and there are sexualities of struggle and choice. The 'invention of sexuality' was not a single event, now lost in a distant past. It is a continuing process in which we are simultaneously acted upon and actors, objects of change, and its subjects.

3

THE MEANINGS OF SEXUAL DIFFERENCE

Q. Was your first partner a man or a woman?
A. I was too polite to ask.

(Interview with the novelist Gore Vidal)

THE BIOLOGICAL IMPERATIVE

Gore Vidal's characteristic response to a mildly cheeky question amuses and perhaps jolts us because in our culture whom we have sex with matters. Gender, a term conventionally deployed to describe the social condition of being male or female, and sexuality, the cultural way of living out our bodily pleasures and desires, have become inextricably linked, with the result that crossing the boundary between proper masculine or feminine behaviour (that is, what is culturally defined as appropriate) sometimes seems the ultimate transgression. We still find it difficult to think about sexuality without taking into account gender; or, to put it more generally, the elaborate facade of sexuality has in large part been built upon the assumption of fundamental differences between men and women, and of male dominance over women. The genital and reproductive distinctions between biological men and biological women have been read not only as necessary but also as sufficient explanation for different sexual needs and desires. They appear as the most basic distinctions between peoples, deeply rooted in our 'animal natures'.

It is one of the peculiarities of us humans that we seek answers to some of our most fundamental questions by looking at the lives of animals. That most despised and feared of all creatures, the rat, has had a high profile in sex research, especially in experimental investigations into the effects of 'male' and 'female' hormones. Many other researchers have found evidence and support for their wildest hypotheses about sexual difference in everything from insects and the humble worm to the sea-side sparrow and rhesus monkeys. In the process, much no doubt has been learnt – especially about animal behaviour. But much remains inexplicable by such methods.

Unfortunately for the simplicities of research, human beings are complex, arbitrary and changeable creatures. We manipulate language constantly to reshape our perceptions of the world – and of sex. We per-form in ways which defy the apparent logic of our external appearances. We blur the edges between masculinity and femininity. We create differences that transcend the differences of gender (of age, race, sexual need); and we construct boundaries that have little logic 'in Nature'. We even change our behaviour in response to moral, political or accidental factors. Yet all the time we like to indulge the fantasy that our sex is the most basic, the most natural, thing about us, and that the relations between men and women are laid down for all eternity, like finger-prints in concrete, by the dictates of our inborn 'nature'. In cultures preoccupied with sexual difference, as most of the sexual cultures around the world still are, such beliefs have crucial social effects: to repeat, the way we think about sex shapes the way we live it. So discussions about the origins and form of the differences between men and women are much more than obscure debates. They are central to the direction of our society.

John Money has noted 'the cultural practice, taken for granted in our culture, of maximizing the differences, behavioral included, between the sexes, rather than maximizing the similarities' (Money 1980: 133). The 'science of sex' cannot be blamed for this, given the deeply embedded cultural assumptions the early sexologists encountered: in many ways they merely theorized what they believed they saw. Moreover, many of them, alive to empirical reality, were eventually anxious to assert the overlap as much as the differences. For Havelock Ellis in the 1930s, sex was 'mutable', its frontiers uncertain, with 'many stages between a complete male and a complete female' (Ellis 1946: 194). Yet at the same time the search for the essentially feminine and the essentially masculine continued, with the inevitable result that sexual differences were stressed at the expense of similarities. Sexology became a weapon in the endemic conflict over the appropriate social relationships and positionings of men and women that was accentuated in the last decades of the nineteenth century and has continued, with varying rhythms and intensity, ever since.

The very definition of the sexual instinct was essentially one derived from male practices and fantasies. Just consider some of the metaphors deployed in writings on sex: overpowering forces, engulfing drives, gushing streams, uncontrollable spasms – such imagery has dominated the Western discourse on sex. Early sexologists drew on this imagery even as they attempted to put it on a more scientific basis. So sex was defined as a 'physiological law', 'a force generated by powerful ferments', a drive 'which cannot be set aside for any sort of social convention', and most graphically of all, 'a volcano that burns down and lays waste all around it; . . . an abyss that devours all honour, substance and health' [1]. The Darwinian revolution in biology, which demonstrated that man was part of the animal world, encouraged the search for the animal in man, and found it in his sex.

Female sexuality was inevitably a problem – an enigma, a 'dark continent' in Freud's famous words – for such views. From the ancient world to the eighteenth century, medical theory taught that there was but one sex, with the female body simply an inverted version of the male. Simultaneously, popular cultural tradition held that female sexuality was voracious, all-devouring and consuming. This has had a significant recent revival in comments (by men) that modern feminism has exhausted and enfeebled men by encouraging female sexual demands. Such an argument probably tells us more about male fears and fantasies than it does about women, but it has to be noted nonetheless as a fanciful and persistent myth. But since the nineteenth century the more conventional view has been to treat female sexuality as fundamentally different but basically complementary to male sexuality: reactive, responsive, brought to life only through some sort of 'reproductive instinct', or kissed into life by the skill of the wooer, the male. Lesbianism has been particularly problematic for theorists of sex precisely because it was an autonomously female sexuality in which men played no part.

The idea that there is a *fundamental* difference between male and female sexual natures has been a powerful one. Even the abundant evidence, building on the observational work of Kinsey and Masters and Johnson, that there is a fundamentally similar physiological response amongst men and women, has not undermined the belief in basic psychosexual differences elsewhere [2].

The idea that there are differences between peoples is not in itself dangerous. What is peculiar about the gender/sexuality nexus is that certain differences have been seen as so fundamental that they become divisions and even antagonisms. At best there is the argument that though men and women may be different they can still be equal. At worst, assumptions about the forceful nature of the male sexual drive have been used to legitimize male domination over women, and to affirm the female destiny of reproduction.

We might think that such beliefs have been sufficiently undermined in recent years, especially through the critiques of modern feminism, to have little credence today. But we would be mistaken. Take the views of some recent writers influential on what became known as the 'New Right' in Britain and North America during the 1980s. Roger Scruton, an English Conservative philosopher, has counterposed what he vividly describes as the 'unbridled ambition of the phallus', eschewing all obligation, to the nature-given role of women to 'quieten what is most vagrant'. For George Gilder, a fervent defender of traditional values, it is only the claims of marriage and the family that can channel the man's 'otherwise disruptive male aggression' into social obligation to fend for his wife and offspring (Scruton 1983, 1986; Gilder 1973). The feminist case against (culturally encoded) male sexual violence is thus transformed into a defence of sexual division *and* traditional morality. For both writers there is a belief in a refractory (male) human nature, threatening disruption unless constrained by moral will and social orthodoxy.

Views such as this found a justification in the 'new synthesis' of sociobiology, through which biological determinism enjoyed a revival in the 1970s and 1980s, and in its sibling, evolutionary psychology, which to some extent had superseded it in influence by the Millennium. Both tendencies have made an important impact, and not only on the

Right. The new prestige enjoyed by the genetic revolution has been deployed by a number of liberal sources to explain the intractability to change of social institutions, and the inevitability of certain givens (such as male/female differences), and some aspects of it have even been used to argue for greater freedom for sexual minorities on the grounds of their biological functionality. We need, therefore, to be alive to the appeal of the new evolutionism – as well as to the dangers I believe to be inherent in it.

Sociobiology was defined by its founding father, E. O. Wilson, as 'the systematic study of the biological basis of all social behavior' (Wilson 1975: 4). It aimed to bridge the gap which had opened up between traditional biological theories on the one hand and social explanations on the other by attempting to demonstrate that there was a key mechanism linking both. This mechanism, in the words of one of Wilson's early enthusiasts, was 'the fundamental law of gene selfishness' (Dawkins 1978: 7). The gene is the basic unit of heredity, defined as a portion of the DNA molecule which affects the development of any trait at the most elementary biochemical level. It carries the code which influences future development. So much may be generally agreed. Where many new evolutionists go further is by arguing – going enthusiastically beyond Wilson's initially more tentative positions – that genes exist for every social phenomenon, so that the random survival of the genes could explain all social practices from economic efficiency and educational attainment to gender divisions and sexual preference. In this mode of thought the fundamental unit is no longer 'the individual', as in classical liberal theory; nor is it 'society', as in the great alternative tradition. The individual is now viewed as little more than a vehicle for the transmission of genes, 'a selfish machine, programmed to do whatever is best for his genes as a whole' (Dawkins 1978: 71). If this is true, then the great conflict between individual and society can be simply dissolved: a continuum exists between the timeless energy of the gene, and the most complex social manifestations, with 'society and nature working in harmony'. So what about apparently social institutions like marriage, parenting, social bonding? They were 'adaptive', in a key term of sociobiology and evolutionary psychology, products not of history or social development but of 'evolutionary necessity'. And what about ideas, ideals, values and beliefs? They are no more than 'enabling mechanisms for survival'.

So, certain aspects of human sexual behaviour, such as male philandering and female coyness, the argument goes, are biological adaptations selected in the infancy of the human race, 100,000, to 600,000 years ago, and have become universal features of human nature, ensuring the propagation of our ancestors' genes. Similarly, rape can be seen as an adaptive strategy, by which otherwise sexually unsuccessful men propagate their genes by mating with fertile women who might otherwise reject them; or parental love can be reduced to a means of successfully ensuring gene survival [3].

Given this certainty, the existence of but two sexes is paradoxically a problem for sociobiology. Sex, E. O. Wilson argues, is an antisocial force in evolution, for it causes difficulty between people. The male/female relationship is one of mutual mistrust and exploitation. Altruism, necessary for gene survival, is more likely when everyone is the same. So why is human reproduction not carried out through parthenogenesis, as it is with some primitive creatures? And why are there two, not three, four or five sexes? 'To be perfectly honest', Cherfas and Gribbin admit, 'nobody knows' (Cherfas and Gribbin 1984: 4). Which is why, they decide, sex is such an enigma. The new evolutionists do, however, offer a working hypothesis which fits in with their overall framework. The most likely reason for sexed reproduction, they have ultimately decided, is that it promotes diversity, the ability to shuffle the genetic pack to hedge bets against an unpredictably changing environment. Two sexes are just enough to ensure the maximum potential genetic recombination. Two sexes also ensure health and hardiness, by mixing the chemical constituents sufficiently to produce immunity against disease. So men's job 'is to provide the means by which females can fight off disease': far from being 'redundant', men are still essential for the future of the human race [4].

Whatever the intricate (and sometimes metaphysical) speculations, one outstanding conclusion flows from all this: 'with respect to sexuality, there is a female human nature and a male human nature, and these natures are extraordinarily different . . .' (Symons 1979: 11). These differences begin and end, it appears, with the evolutionary characteristics of the ova and testes. Because males have an almost infinite number of sperm (millions with each ejaculation), while women have a very restricted supply of eggs (around 400 per lifetime), it is deduced that men have an evolutionary propulsion towards spreading their seed to ensure diversity and reproductive success, and hence towards promiscuity, while women have an equal interest in reserving energy, an instinct for conservation, and hence a leaning towards monogamy. From this can be deduced the explanations for all the other supposedly fundamental differences: greater competition between men than between women, a greater male tendency towards polygamy and jealousy whereas women are 'more malleable' and amenable, and a greater sexual will and arousal potential in men than in women:

> Among all peoples copulation is considered to be essentially a service or favor that women render to men, and not vice versa, regardless of which sex desires or is thought to desire greater pleasure from sexual intercourse.
>
> (Symons 1979: 27–8)

There is clearly a great intellectual attraction in such evolutionary explanations: they provide clarity where social scientists may see complexity, certainty where others recognize only contingency. There is also a certain political logic in the vogue for evolutionary theories: they provide an explanation for certain apparently intractable social problems in a conservative cultural climate, for example, why men are so reluctant to change, why homosexuals are different from heterosexuals. Such theories also – and this is a prize attribute – seem to speak to widespread, commonsense beliefs about the naturalness of sexual divisions. They go with, rather than against, the grain of popular prejudice. But if they can claim to explain some things (love at first sight 'may simply be the powerful response of the body to the scent of a very different set of histo-compatibility antigens'; homosexuality may be necessary to encourage altruistic concern for the offspring of siblings), they cannot generally or convincingly explain others (why there are variations between different cultures, for example, or why history frequently undergoes rapid social change). The new evolutionism is also, as an approach, ultimately deeply conservative in its implications, for if the explanation of what we do, socially and sexually, lies in the haphazard collision of genes, then there is little we can do to change things: bend the twig a little here, unbend it there, but not too much either way in case the whole branch breaks off. If, as H. J. Eysenck and Glenn Wilson reaffirm, there is 'a strong, underlying biological source for the widely differing sexual attitudes we observe when we look at men and women' (Eysenck and Wilson 1979: 9), then feminist demands – or even liberal reforms – are utopian. As some earlier advocates of biological determinism put it, in the context of an earlier upsurge of feminist activity, 'What was decided among the prehistoric protozoa cannot be annulled by Act of Parliament'. There seems little argument about that.

Some or all of this may of course be true. The problem is that while evidence from biology, natural history, or the postulated early history of mankind may be suggestive, it cannot be conclusive. It may be impossible finally to disprove a sociobiological or evolutionary psychology hypothesis – who knows what 'science' will turn up? – but it is equally difficult to prove it. In the real world of sexuality in which we live, things are a little more complex than the high priests of the 'sexual tradition' (amongst whom we must now count the new evolutionists) like to think. The most ardent advocates of biological determinism generally display three characteristic modes of argument: argument by analogy; a reliance, amounting almost to an intellectual tyranny, on 'average statements'; and finally what I shall call, for want of a better phrase, the 'black hole' hypothesis. They are all fraught with difficulties.

(1) Argument by analogy

This assumes that by observing animals in the wild we can crack the code of our civilization. A new emphasis on observing animals in their natural habitat during the inter-war years was one of the roots of sociobiology. E. O. Wilson devoted most of his first attempts at a synthesis to insects and birds. The trouble here is that despite all efforts at neutral observation, human prejudices insensibly creep in. As Rose *et al.* put it:

> Again and again, in order to support their claims to the inevitability of a given feature of the human order, biological determinists seek to imply the universality of their claims. If male dominance exists in humans, it is because it exists also in baboons, in lions, in ducks, or whatever. The ethological literature is replete with accounts of 'harem-keeping' by baboons, the male lion's domination of 'his' pride, 'gang-rape' in mallard ducks, 'prostitution' in humming birds.
>
> (Rose *et al.* 1984: 158)

It should hardly need saying that what is happening here is the attribution of highly coloured social explanations to animal behaviour. Why should groupings of female animals be seen as harems? They could equally well be seen, for all the counter-evidence available, as prototypes of women's consciousness-raising groups. To say that perhaps evokes a smile. But so should the circular argument by which explanations drawn from human experience are attributed to animals and then used to justify social divisions in the present.

Evolutionary psychology partly recognizes that by moving away from explanations rooted in animal behaviour – in favour of evidence provided by our genetic inheritance, and by theorized originary Adams and Eves on the prehistoric savannah. But this narrative is itself disrupted by dogmatic assumption that explanations lie in 'reproductive strategies' to ensure gene survival. Such theorizations deny human agency and creativity in favour of a hypothetical evolutionary metahistory.

(2) The tyranny of averages

Explanations based on averages provide another seductive but dangerous approach. On *average,* men may be more sexually active than women. Male homosexuals *may* be more promiscuous than female homosexuals. This *may* have something to do with the genes. It may equally have something to do with culture: greater opportunities for male sexual expression, and for choice of partners, for example. More fundamentally, to say that on average men have more sexual activity than women is tantamount to saying that some women are more sexually active than some men. Average statements are both true and not particularly useful. Yet they carry an enormous weight, in part at least because we prefer clear-cut divisions to ambiguity. Nature herself, however, can be very ambivalent, as the very idea of 'averages' suggests. Why aren't we?

(3) The 'black hole' hypothesis

The 'black hole' hypothesis – the assumption that if there are mysterious effects, there must be something unknown but determinate out there which can explain them – is the final resort for those who can find no other explanation for sexual differences. If all else fails to explain human phenomena, then a biological cause, even if as yet it is undetected, must exist. If more men than women are in top jobs, then biology surely explains it. If society is resistant to the politics of feminism, then it must be because it goes against human nature. If the causes of homosexuality can be explained neither by sociology nor psychoanalysis, then biology (hormones, instincts, a 'gay gene' or the 'gay brain' . . .) must explain it. There is a classic example of this at the conclusion of the final report of the Kinsey Institute on homosexuality, *Sexual Preferences*. The authors carefully explore the lack of evidence for a single cause of homosexuality, and conclude that there is no evidence for one in sociology or psychology. But instead of then testing the hypothesis (which Kinsey himself had endorsed) that homosexuality was not, therefore, a unitary condition, with single roots (and in any case was no more worthy of aetiological explanation than its supposed opposite, heterosexuality), the authors conclude that there must be a biological explanation. This, in the context of the book, is empty speculation. The 'solution' owes more to the continuing prestige of biological sciences than evidence. It positively invited a further generation of search for the gay gene or gay brain [5]. The so-called discovery of both seemed to justify the search – only for the evidence to crumble when subject to detailed interrogation. But as ever, biology is called on to fill a gap which social explanations have been unwilling, or unable, to fill.

I have no desire to minimize the importance of biology. Biological capacities clearly provide the potentiality out of which so much that is human is shaped. The body, in its full corporality, provides the locus, and sets the limit for social activities. On the body are inscribed our differences as men and women. Copulation, reproduction, nurturance and death are clearly biological in origin and provide the parameters of human existence. Less cosmic biological factors equally have social effects. Genetic differences (amongst men and amongst women, as well as between them) can affect physical appearances, size, strength, longevity, the colour of hair and eyes. Differential production of hormones can affect sexual maturation, distribution of body hair, fat deposition and muscular development. These are not unimportant as they are elaborated in complex cultural codes which lay down the appropriate or inappropriate physical appearance and behaviour of each gender. But it is, ultimately, the social meaning that we give to these differences that is of real importance. If 'the biological differences between the sexes are actually minute when compared with the similarities' (Nicholson 1984: 6) and in fact, only one gene out of 100,000 needed to make up each person distinguishes men from women, then the critical markers that we conventionally use to demarcate difference need to be re-evaluated.

Anatomical differences are apparently the most basic of all. It is on the presence or absence of the male or female organs that gender is immediately assigned at birth. Yet, the possession of a penis or vagina cannot be a universally applicable standard. In birds, the male does not have a penis; other animals have only 'intromittent organs', such as claspers in sharks and dogfish [6]. Even amongst us humans the meanings of these very real organs are not transparent. The vagina can be conceived of as passive, or as all-devouring. The clitoris has been conceptualized as no more than a 'vestigial phallus', and as the site of women's multi-orgasmic potential. The penis has an even more supercharged symbolic value in our culture. Its 'thrusting', 'forceful', 'penetrative' nature has been seen as the very model of active male sexuality. But, as Richard Dyer has sharply pointed out, there is a marked discrepancy between this symbolism and the way the penis is often experienced:

> Male genitals are fragile, squashy, delicate things . . . penises are only little things (even big ones) without much staying power, pretty if you can learn to see them like that, but not magical or mysterious or powerful in themselves, that is, not objectively full of real power.
>
> (Dyer 1985: 30–1)

The significance we give to the male and female organs is important both socially and psychologically. If we follow the insights of psychoanalysis, then the existence or absence of the male penis (that is, the fear or fantasy of castration) is critical for the negotiation of the Oedipal crisis, and for the acquisition or non-acquisition of psychological masculinity and femininity, the very organization of sexual difference. But the critical meanings we assign to them are, according to Freud, demanded by culture and do not arise straightforwardly from the biology alone.

The same potential ambiguity exists over two other, less obvious markers: the chromosomal make-up of men and women, and hormonal patterns. The existence, firstly, of chromosomal differences is well known. The distinction is the one made in international sporting competitions for defining the sexes, where competitors, in women's athletic events particularly, have to undergo a sex chromosome test (Archer and Lloyd 1982: 47). Human beings have in the nucleus of every cell in their body 46 chromosomes: twenty-two pairs, and two sex chromosomes. In females these sex chromosomes are identical (XX); but in males one is an incomplete structure, carrying little genetic material (the Y chromosome: men generally have an XY pairing).

The difficulty is that these are not absolute markers. Sometimes chromosomes do not separate during cell division in the usual way, giving rise to XXY, X, XXX, or XYY patterns: are they male or female? Sometimes there are individuals whose chromosomes say one thing, and their appearance another: males in that they have XY chromosomes, and possess testes which secrete the male hormone; but ambiguous in that they have not, through congenital androgen insensitivity, become externally masculinized. Even Nature, in her wisdom, apparently makes mistakes. Abnormalities such as these, Archer and Lloyd concluded, 'illustrate the complex and precarious nature of the development process' – and hence of the division between the sexes (Archer and Lloyd 1982: 69).

Similarly, and secondly, the importance assigned to hormones, the chemical messengers secreted by the glands, has been exaggerated. The main hormone produced by the testes is testosterone; this, together with hormones of the same general type, are called *androgens,* the 'male hormones'. The main hormones produced by the ovaries are oestrogen and progesterone (the 'female hormones'). These hormones are undoubtedly important for development: testosterone produces important changes at adolescence, including a deepening voice and the appearance of body hair. The rise of oestrogen levels in girls at puberty encourages breast development, fat redistribution and the beginning of the menstrual cycle. But even so, we are not talking of uniquely male and female possessions. Ovaries and testes each produce all three hormones, and the adrenal glands secrete androgens in both sexes. What differs is the ratio. Again there is no absolute divide. As Kinsey put it some time ago:

> The fact that hormones are produced in the gonads is, without further evidence, no reason for believing that they are the primary agents controlling those capacities of the nervous system on which sexual response depends.

> (Kinsey *et al.* 1953: 728–9)

Hormones, no more than chromosomes, are decisive in shaping social and psychic sexual differences.

SEXUALITY AND SOCIAL RELATIONS

Biological determinism insists on the fixity of our sexualities, on their resilience in the face of all efforts at modification. Social and historical explanations, on the other hand, assume a high degree of fluidity and flexibility in 'human nature', in its potentiality for change – not overnight, not by individual acts of will, but in the long grind of history and through the complexities and agencies of social interaction. The evidence of other cultures, and of different periods of our own, shows that there are many different ways of being 'men' and 'women', alternative ways of living social and sexual life. The experience of our own recent past has shown the powerful ways in which an energetic social movement – of feminism – with little institutional support can influence and in many cases transform sexual relations. Imagine the power of rapid social change in the past. Our growing awareness of other cultures should make us more attentive to alternative forms of interaction – not least because through the perspective of cultural difference and change we can begin to reflect on the historical contingency of our own 'human nature', and question the supposed fixity of our own positions as 'men' and 'women'.

The overwhelming evidence suggests that sexuality is subject to an enormous degree of socio-cultural moulding, to the extent that, as Plummer has suggested, 'sexuality has no meaning other than that given to it in social situations' (Plummer 1975: 32). But to put it like this does not, of course, resolve difficulties; it merely pushes them along a rather different path. For if sex and sexual differences are social in form, we still need to know where we can set the limits of purely social explanations, what the boundaries against cultural moulding are. Is sex entirely a matter of social naming? Is there a complete interchangeability of roles between men and women? Are our sexual natures infinitely plastic, 'unbelievably malleable' in the famous words of Margaret Mead? Such questions inevitably come to mind, and it must be admitted that we are still quite unsure of the appropriate answers. We know what our sexual natures are not: they are not eternally fixed, biologically determined, and unchangeable. We are not so certain what they are.

There is a real danger therefore of confronting an inadequate bio-logical essentialism with an equally inadequate sociological essentialism, in which the malleability of sexuality is always at the bidding of deterministic social imperatives. For the enormously influential social anthropologists of the inter-war years it was not human nature but the 'cultural configuration' that was the main object of concern. This was a real gain in that it forced a rethink of many cherished sociological 'truths'. But there were, nevertheless, real problems with the cultural relativism that emerged. Each culture presented itself as a necessary and inexplicable set of differences from others. History, development and change were not issues high on the agenda. Each society, moreover, was seen as imposing itself on its inhabitants as a totality in which all social positions were *necessary* responses to societal demands. This type of argument has been taken up by many later writers to argue for the functionality of sex roles. Individuals 'accept and reproduce', Weinstein and Platt wrote, 'the patterns of behavior required by society', with the family as the main conduit for this social moulding, and neatly complementary 'social roles' as the necessary result (Weinstein and Platt 1969: 6). There does not seem to be much room for manoeuvre in this. Not only is society seen as the prime mover, but individuals, we must presume, are blank sheets, *tabula rasa*, on which are imprinted the required characteristics needed to make that society function adequately. Society organizes a sexual division of labour to fulfil its demands – in reproduction, nurturance, employment, household activities, and sex. It even creates deviant and stigmatized social roles – for example, the 'role' of homosexuals in our culture – both to provide slots for those who cannot quite fit in, and to act as a warning to the rest of society of the awesome effects of stepping out of line.

Such arguments obviously have an appeal. They offer an elegant expla-nation for the obvious differences and divisions we see around us. But there is a problem with any theory which endows 'society' with a conscious will, and which believes that all the parts fit together like a marvellous clockwork: where do people and their subjective wills and agency come in? Moreover, there is a curiously paradoxical result of this stress on social moulding. In emphasizing the social as the prime mover, certain characteristics of 'nature' are not questioned. More specifically, in most socially deterministic accounts the necessity for a sexual division of labour along lines of anatomical differences is not challenged but reaffirmed.

This is clear in the work of Margaret Mead, who battled harder than most to suggest the flexibility of human nature. In *Sex and Temperament in Three Primitive Societies* she found a great range of sex variations in New Guinea (Mead 1948: 279–80). The Arapesh had no strong idea of sex as an overpowering force in either men or women, and both sexes had qualities that could be called 'maternal'. Amongst the Mundugumor, on the other hand, both men and women were positively sexed and aggressive. In the third tribe, the Tchambuli, there was a full reversal of the sex attitudes of our own culture, with women as dominant and men emotionally dependent. In a later work, summarizing the evidence, Mead suggested that 'In every known society, mankind has elaborated the biological division of labour into forms often very remotely related to the original biological differences that provided the original clues . . . sometimes one quality has been assigned to one sex, sometimes to the other' (Mead 1949: 7). Yet, at the same time as the possibility of social moulding is reaffirmed, those 'original clues' assume a critical importance. For if human society is to survive, she argues, 'it must have a pattern of social life that comes to terms with the differences between the sexes' (Mead 1949: 163). What are these? Reproductive capacities are clearly different between men and women, and even the development of reproductive technologies is unlikely to change this fundamentally. On the basis of these differences, cultures have elaborated separated roles – for parenting, nurturance, work and household organization. But as Mead's own writings show, the form of those roles varies enormously, with men and women interchangeable in the qualities we describe as 'maternal' and 'paternal'. If social roles are so flexible, if there is no necessary connection between reproduction, gender and sexual attributes, it is not clear why sharp sexual dichotomies should be so crucially necessary – unless we make a prior assumption about their inevitability. It is difficult to avoid the conclusion that in the end Mead takes for granted the prime significance of anatomy: anatomical difference guarantees the roles required by society. This may be true, but why this should be so is never questioned. Surely it is of prime importance to know why so many cultures have chosen anatomy as the fundamental basis of our social destinies.

We need to go beyond the simplicities of some of these explanations. I want to suggest particularly that neither is 'society' as unified and total in its impact as these theories suggest, nor are the lines of difference so clear-cut and decisive. If we look at what we mean by 'society' we find that in practice all social theory confirms the complexity of social relationships, the 'multiple realities' through which we negotiate our everyday lives. 'Society' is not a whole governed by a coherent set of determinants, but an intricate web of institutions, beliefs, habits, ideologies and social practices that have no *a priori* unity and whose actual relationships have to be unravelled rather than taken as read. If we transfer this view of 'the social' to sexual activities, we will see that far from 'society' moulding 'sexuality', in any straightforward way, what we describe as sexual is constructed through a complexity of social relations, each of which has a different view of what constitutes sex and appropriate sexual behaviour. The modern apparatus of sexuality, Michel Foucault has suggested, is heterogeneous, including: 'discourses, institutions, architectural arrangements, regulations, laws, administrative measures, scientific statements, philosophic propositions, morality, philanthropy, etc.' (Foucault 1980: 194). All of these together make up what we define as sexuality, but they clearly do not and cannot all say the same things, or address us in identical ways.

There exists in the world of sexuality a variety of different and often contradictory accounts of what it is to be sexual: organized sets of meanings ('discourses'), articulated through a variety of different languages, and anchored in a dense network of social activities. Traditional Christian concepts of sexual behaviour, for example, rely on certain assumptions about human nature – that it is unregenerate or corrupt, that the division of the sexes was preordained, that sexual activity is only justified by reproduction or love. These beliefs are laid down in a set of statements – biblical interpretations, commentaries, canon law, sermons. They are generalized through a language of certitude and morality, which divides the sinners from the saved, the moral from the immoral. These meanings are embodied in institutions which work to reinforce beliefs and behaviours: churches, the privileged position of parenthood, the practices of confession or testimony before God, the existence of religious schools, the sacraments of baptism and marriage, even, in many countries, the legal system. The totality of these discourses and practices constructs 'subject positions' in which the moral elite can recognize themselves as truly among the chosen, and the sinful as beyond the hope of redemption. Individuals are shaped, and shape themselves, in relationship to such pre-existing sets of meaning (in the example given here they are Christian; they could equally be Islamic, Hindu, Judaic, or even secular, as in the Soviet effort to create the new 'socialist man'), which seek to regulate and control their behaviour according to firm and consciously and unconsciously imbibed rules.

It is here that the idea of the 'script', used by some interactionist sociologists to account for the way we take our sexual meanings, provides a powerful, if inevitably ambiguous, metaphor: 'Scripts specify, like blueprints', John Gagnon has suggested, 'the whos, whats, whens, wheres and whys for given types of activity . . . It is like a blueprint or roadmap or recipe, giving directions . . . ' [7]. In this sense, scripts act in rather the same way as the earlier sociological concepts of roles. We do not, of course, follow absolutely these guidelines, or we would all be the same, and 'immorality', deviance or transgression would scarcely exist. But the 'scripts' laid down in certain social practices set the parameters within which individual choices are available; and there are oppositional as well as regulatory scripts. There are a variety of possible sexual meanings coexisting at any one time.

In the Christian West people have been subjected to a host of conflicting and often contradictory definitions. Medicine since the nineteenth century has worked hard to displace religion as the major force in the regulation of sexuality. Its language speaks less of morality and more of the 'natural' and 'unnatural', healthy and sick sexualities; its institutional focus is the clinic, hospital or psychiatrist's couch (Michel Foucault was not the first to suggest an analogy between the confessional mode and the talking cure of psychoanalysis: Freud himself made the same connection). Then there are the languages of law, education, anthropology, sociology and politics, all of which speak in carefully differentiated tones about sexuality: is it a product of criminality, nurture, cultural variation, political choice? And of course there are the counter-discourses, the reverse and often militant languages, the new 'sexual stories' of the new sexual movements and communities organized around sexual identities and practices. We live in a world of rival and often contradictory descriptions and definitions.

The emergence of clear-cut sexual differences is therefore a prolonged process for each individual subject, learned in all the complexities of social life. Family life provides models, though these are by no means clear-cut. Schools convey clear messages, though not always in the same direction. Peer group assessment guards the barricades against social deviance. Rituals of courtship, sexual initiation, even sexual violence affirm divisions. Desires and choices of partner secure the path of normality or the road to unorthodox behaviour. Media representations construct the images of desirable identities. Religious and moral and political involvements help organize adult ways of life. Even chance brings its wayward influence. It is in response to all these influences – and many more – that we construct our subjectivities, our sense of who we are, how we came to where we are, where we want to go: our identities as men and women, heterosexual and homosexual, or whatever, are a product of complex processes of definition and self-definition in a complex arrangement of social relations.

On the surface, at least, this suggests that male and female identities, far from being fixed for all eternity by natural attributes, are rather fragile and haphazard, subject to a variety of influences and often torn by contradictions. For instance, people learn early on in Western societies that to be a 'man' is to be not a homosexual. Male homosexuality has been stigmatized through several centuries as effeminate, an inversion of gender, precisely 'unmanly'. Yet we also know that many 'real men' do see themselves as homosexual, and that from the 1970s there was a general reaction in the male gay world against an automatic association of homosexuality with effeminacy. Conventional views about what it is to be a man often conflict with sexual desires and (probably) sexual activities: yet for many gay men the two are held in tension. The sexuality of women provides another example: women have been traditionally defined as having a sexuality which is responsive, nurturant and closely associated with reproduction. But over the past few decades, women's bodies have been increasingly sexualized in the media and through representations generally. The same woman can be addressed in the pages of a glossy magazine both as an efficient homemaker, caring and domestic, and as a *femme fatale*, sexual and alluring, with no sense that the different definitions may be in conflict or may have confusing effects. And, of course, women have sought to take control of their own sexualities, to define themselves as autonomous erotic beings. We hold together in our minds and in our sexual makeups a host of changing, and often warring accounts of ourselves, our motives, our wishes and desires, and our needs.

But the social world does demand distinctions, and creates boundaries. 'Masculinity' and 'femininity' may not be unified concepts. They are

fraught with conflicting and contradictory messages, and they have
different meanings in different contexts. They do not mean the same
thing in formal social documents or legal codes as they do in popular
prejudice. They mean different things in different class, geographical
and racial milieux. And yet, whatever the qualifications we make,
they exist not only as powerful ideas but as critical social divides. We do
it in different ways at different times but we all the time divide people
into 'men' and 'women'. More than this, we are not speaking of simple,
meaningless differences: we are in fact referring to power differentials
and to historical situations where socially and practically men have
had the power to define women. Maleness and male sexuality remain
the norms by which we judge women. This does not mean that male
definitions are simply accepted; on the contrary, there are constant battles
over sexual meanings at individual and collective levels, and there are
different types of masculinities – hegemonic, subordinate, marginalized
– which shift over time, as they respond to changing pressures and
struggles. But the battles are against, and within the limits set, by the
dominant terms. These in turn are encoded via a social privileging
of particular relationships – in marriage and family arrangements and
a host of other social institutions and activities, through which gender,
and sexual, identities are constructed and constantly reaffirmed and
performed.

Gender and sexuality, therefore, are less the expressions of some
underlying truths about human nature. They are things we do in defined
situations, things we do over and over again, small acts incessantly
repeated, productions which, as Judith Butler has suggested, 'create
the effect of the natural, the original, and the inevitable' (Butler 1990:
x; see also Butler 1993). If we accept this radical view, then there is
nothing out there which explains everything: there is no 'there' there.
There are only the repetitive acts, imitations of imitations, through which
gendered and sexualized identities are performatively produced. From
this perspective, heterosexuality and homosexuality are not emanations
of the genes or hormones or anything else: they are regulative fictions
and ideals through which conformities are generated, reinforced and
'normalized' by constant reiterations. That does not mean that the body
is a fiction. The norms are inscribed on the body in a variety of ways
through the relations and rituals of power which prescribe and proscribe
appearance, physicality, who and what is desirable, and so on. The point

is that while sex could not exist without the body, sexuality does not emanate effortlessly from the body.

Perhaps most of this takes place on a level where its subtleties escape our conscious notice. But its weight can be determining. Researchers have shown the extreme pressures to conform to accepted sexual divisions and heterosexual arrangements that exist and are constantly reinforced amongst children, adolescents and adults alike through language, ritual and interaction. Differences are institutionalized and reaffirmed throughout social life – through parental practices, the education processes, peer pressures, work practices ('sexual harassment') and street conventions ('wolf whistles'), to routine rituals in bars and other social activities. Despite all the changes that have taken place, now on a global scale, male sexuality as culturally defined continues to provide the norm and, not surprisingly, female sexuality continues to be the problem. Males, in *becoming* men, take up positions in power relations in which they acquire the ability to define women. That does not mean these power relations cannot be challenged, nor that gendered sexual relations are fixed for all time. But it does mean we have to start by recognizing the entrenched patterns that continue to delimit the domains of sexuality.

SEXUALITY AND THE UNCONSCIOUS

Two major points should stand out from the discussion so far. First, we need to recognize, more readily than we are inclined to do, that gender and sexual identities are not pre-given, automatic or fixed. They are on the contrary both socially organized *and* contingent. They are also relational. Masculinity and femininity each exist only because of the existence of the other. They are shifting and changing definitions, locked together in an apparently inevitable but all the time changing dance of life and death. Secondly, we seem unable to escape our strong investment in sexual difference, a difference where women are perennially subordinate to men. In part, no doubt, this historical continuity can be explained by reference to the considerable power it does give to men. Advocates of the existence across all cultures of structures of patriarchal power would see this as a sufficient explanation. It cannot explain, however, either the deep commitment we seem to have to sexual difference, or the strain that is evident in many people's lives, men and women, as they strive to maintain it. Sexual difference is apparently necessary *and* precarious, fundamental yet provisional. How then do we recognize ourselves in these social categories? Why do we invest so much in what appears to modern sexual theory so ephemeral? Why are sexual differences apparently so inessential yet so permanent and resilient? It is at this point that insights can be gained from another theoretical approach, that of psychoanalysis, the theory of the dynamic unconscious and of desire.

Psychoanalysis has made a critical contribution to the theorization of sex during the past century or so, though its impact has often been ambiguous and contradictory. Like so many other of the great intellectual preoccupations of the twentieth century (Marxism, democracy and nationalism spring to mind), it has different meanings in different contexts. Freud's own work provides a treasure chest for varying inter-pretations, while the work of the many who claim to be his legitimate successors takes us down many highways and byways, often to a destination that bears little relationship to what Freud said, or meant, or wanted to believe. It is therefore hazardous in the extreme to venture to describe a 'true Freud'. A more interesting and adventurous route is to look at the way in which recent reinterpretations of Freud have offered a challenge to the orthodoxies of the sexual tradition. Here the critical contribution has come from feminist appropriations of psycho-analysis, drawing initially on the work of the French analyst, Jacques Lacan, and on the investigations of infancy of Melanie Klein, but developing a range of perspectives in which the 'perverse' returns to challenge the normalizing tendencies of the analytic tradition.

The importance of psychoanalysis lies in the fact that it precisely did not assume sexuality as an unproblematic category (Coward 1983). Rather, it can be argued, psychoanalysis proposed a radical re-examination of the concept of sexuality, questioning the centrality of sexual reproduction and the rigid distinctions between men and women. The significance of this approach is that it challenges essentialist views, and problematizes the pre-given nature of sexual difference, at the same time as it recognizes the power of unconscious meanings. This is an important extension and development of Freud's own work. Freud was in fact very clear on the problematic nature of concepts of masculinity and femininity, believing them to be amongst the most difficult known to science. Following from these early Freudian insights, there are three crucial strands in the contemporary appropriation of psychoanalysis. First, there is the theory of the unconscious itself, the very core of psychoanalysis. The psycho-analytic tradition proposes that individuals are not predetermined products of biological imperatives, nor are they the effects simply of social relations. There is a psychic realm – the unconscious – with its own dynamic, rules and history, where the biological possibilities of the body acquire meaning. Chodorow has put this clearly:

> We live an embodied life; we live with those genital and reproductive organs and capacities, those hormones and chromosomes, that locate us physiologically as male and female. But . . . there is nothing self-evident about this biology. How anyone understands, fantasizes about, symbolizes, internally represents, or feels about her or his physiology is a product of development and experience in the family and not a direct product of the biology itself.
>
> (Chodorow 1980: 18)

The unconscious is a sphere of conflict: between ideas, wishes, and desires – above all sexual desires – denied access to conscious life by the force of mental repression, yet 'returning' all the time to disrupt consciousness in the form of dreams, slips of the tongue, jokes, neurotic symptoms or perverse behaviour. What fundamentally constitutes the unconscious are those wishes and desires which are repressed in the face of the demands of reality, and in particular the repressed, incestuous desires of infancy: 'What is unconscious in mental life is also what is infantile' [8].

This leads to the second point: to a theorization of sexual difference. Identities – as men and women – and the organization of desires and object choices – as heterosexual, homosexual, or whatever – are not laid down automatically at birth. They are a product of psychic struggle and conflict as the initial 'blob of humanity', with its undifferentiated, polymorphously perverse sexuality, and bisexual nature (object-choice is not pre-given), negotiates the hazard-strewn path to a precarious maturity. The child negotiates the phases of initial development where different parts of the body become focuses of erotic excitement (the oral, anal, phallic and genital phases), advancing through the dawning recognition of 'castration' (the presence or absence of the male organ) to the drama of the Oedipus crisis, in which the young person struggles with incestuous desires for the mother and the father, to an eventual identification with the 'appropriate parent' of the same sex. Through this 'epic' struggle the undifferentiated infant finally becomes a little man or a little woman. This is of course a schematic description which does little justice to the subtle intricacies of Freud's final accounts. There is no inevitable progress to the altar of proper behaviour. If the process 'worked' automatically there would be no ambiguity about gender, no homosexuality, fetishism, transvestism, and so on. I offer the description to underline the point that for Freud, attaining sexual identity, and the soldering together of identity and desire (who we are, and what we need and lack), is a struggle that we all have to enter and that by no means ends in a victorious capture of the position allotted to us by reason of our anatomy, or the demands of culture.

On the other hand, as Freud notoriously wrote, 'Anatomy is destiny' (Freud 1916–17: 178), and this is the core of the objections to Freud's theories from the first and ever since. The phrase appears to underpin the intractability of our social arrangements, to justify sexual division, to impose a tyranny of the body over the mind. There is, however, an alternative way of seeing the importance of anatomy: as symbolically important, representative of sexual differences, which acquire meaning only in culture. In recent psychoanalytic writings, the penis, or rather its symbolic representative, the phallus, is seen as the prime marker in relation to which meaning is shaped. It is the mark of difference, representing power differences existing in the 'symbolic order', the realm of language, meaning and culture, and of history (and therefore, potentially, of change) [9]. If this is in any way an accurate account, then what the child acquires in its access to the order of meaning at the Oedipal moment is a growing awareness of the *cultural* importance of the male organ for subsequent sexual difference and social position. Thus the threat of castration to the boy (if you don't behave I'll cut your thing off . . .) or the culturally produced belief in a 'castration' that has already taken place for the girl (who does not possess a 'thing') become of decisive psychic significance. The terror of castration propels the young boy and young girl *differently* through the crisis. Both have to break with the primal connection with their mother, but they break with it differently: the boy through an identification with his father and eventual transference of his love for his mother into a desire for other women (this is what a man is, and does); the girl in a much more difficult and long-drawn process to confirm her identification with the mother and transform her desire to have a penis into a desire to receive the favour of the penis from another (that is, to be a woman receptive to a man).

What matters in this is not so much the detail – which in its crude outline can occasionally seem risible – as the attempt it reveals to show how sexed identities are shaped in a complex human process through which anatomical differences acquire meaning in unconscious life. Our destinies are shaped not so much by the differences themselves but by their meaning, which is socially given and psychically elaborated. But a third point emerges from this: that identities are not only precarious acquisitions, they are provisional ones, 'imaginary closures', which are subject to disruptions all the time, through the eruption of unconscious elements, repressed desires not fully or finally extinguished by the Oedipal drama. For Freud, to be human was to be divided, to be constantly 'decentred', swayed by forces outside conscious control. And at the heart of this fractured subjectivity are the ambiguous meanings of masculinity and femininity:

> For psychology, the contrast between the sexes fades away into one between activity and passivity, in which we far too readily identify activity with maleness and passivity with femaleness, a view which is by no means universally confirmed in the animal kingdom.
>
> (Freud 1930: 106, note 3)

At this point Freud can clearly be seen as a precursor of those contemporary accounts which seek to question the fixity of our human nature, and the rigidity of gendered divisions. The phallus as the signifier of difference, and of male dominance, can be subverted – but at what cost?

THE CONSEQUENCES OF DIFFERENCE

We now have two terms with which to challenge the rigidities of biological determinism: 'the social', a web of institutions, relationships and beliefs, and 'the unconscious', which in many ways mediates between social imperatives and biological possibilities, while having a history of its own. Our sexual identities – as men or women, normal or abnormal, heterosexual or homosexual – are constructed from the diverse materials we negotiate in our life courses, limited by our biological inheritance, altered by contingency, social regulation and control, and subject to constant disruptions from unconscious wishes and desires. Yet at the same time we do not seem able easily to escape the differences between the sexes. As Denise Riley observes:

> There is a truth in Freud's 'anatomy is destiny' which is unshakeable. Anatomy, *given everything as it is*, points us irresistibly along certain paths, to certain choices.
>
> (Riley 1983: 4)

The pre-existing structures of gender/sexual difference, the subject positions they prescribe and describe necessarily limit the free play of desire *and* the pursuit of other differences, other ways of being human. We are locked into positions whose uncertainties we can acknowledge but whose compelling attractions we seem unable to avoid.

This is what sustains the structures of 'compulsory heterosexuality', which remains the governing assumption, the regulative ideal, the social and cultural matrix which underpin the gendered order and differentiate our sexual cultures into the acceptable and the dubious or completely unacceptable. But having said that, which suggests the impermeable nature of social structures, we also need to recognize the undoubted reality in the contemporary world of measurable change in relations between men and women, and in attitudes towards sexuality. How can such persistent structures of difference be at the same time obviously susceptible to subversion or transformation? How do we draw up the balance sheet between on the one hand an awareness of determinism by structures which are both conscious and unconscious, and on the other hand the historical fact of individual and collective agency which has transparent achievements?

Much recent scholarship, heavily influenced by feminist debates, has sought to demonstrate the intractable nature of male-dominated heterosexuality. The structuring of sexuality itself is seen as constitutive of gender inequality, across the whole social spectrum from the most private to the most public. There is a (hetero) sexuality of organizations and work as there is a (hetero) sexuality of the bedroom. The sexuality of organizations is shaped along several key dimensions, for example: the verbal (who can say what, when and how); the spatial (who does what, where, the spoken or unspoken hierarchies that shape these decisions); and the physical (how we present ours bodies, for whose approval and gaze). In these situations we *work* at our sexualities, but generally in conditions of inequality between men and women, and the 'normal' and the 'transgressor' (Adkins 1995; Hearn *et al*. 1989; Witz *et al*. 1996).

The question of male sexual violence against women can from this perspective be seen as an extension of a pervasive culture. Such violence is endemic, enacted in a series of sexualized situations from adult rape to child abuse, from sexual harassment at work to domestic violence. If we reject, as I believe we should, the belief that this violence is the inevitable by-product of an inherently aggressive masculinity, and recognize it instead, in Rosalind Coward's words, as 'the ritualistic enactment of cultural meaning about sex' (Coward 1984: 239) then we must find the explanation in the social and psychic conditions in which masculinity is acquired. These are multiple and complex, and not susceptible to simple resolutions. Sex, as we have seen, is a vehicle for a variety of feelings and needs. But for men, Eardley has argued:

> it becomes heavily charged because of the emotional illiteracy which is part and parcel of male socialisation. So often sex then becomes a bottleneck of pent-up and misdirected yearnings, frustrations and anger . . . The pressure of this mass of undigested and unexperienced emotion which clusters around sexuality is perhaps what gives the myth of male urgency its subjective power for men.
>
> (Eardley 1985: 101)

Such an explanation is no doubt partial and inadequate, but it is useful for indicating the blend of factors that do indeed lie at the heart of male aggressiveness, ranging from psychic repression and the conditions of family life to social expectations concerning male behaviour [10].

But if this is agreed, and male sexual violence is not at all a product of an unproblematic biology but of complex social practices and psychic structuring, the changes needed to transform the relations between men and women can only be brought about by equally complex processes, ranging from new methods of child-rearing to radically different economic, legal and social conditions for women. Some remain sceptical that this can be done in any useful timescale. For many, sexuality and gender inequalities remain too locked together to give rise to great optimism for rapid change.

For other theorists of sexuality, however (and I include myself amongst them), the really remarkable fact is the reality of recent change, on a global scale. We must acknowledge firmly and clearly the weight of traditional structures, the miseries of embedded inequalities and injustices, the backlashes as well as the advances. Sexuality remains a domain of appalling violence, pain and disease, a landscape of uneven power relations. This is not surprising, because as I have argued sexuality has become a terrain in which a variety of battles are fought, to constitute what is acceptable or unacceptable, right or wrong. That will go on. But sexuality has also become a focus for other things too: for the articulation of identity and collective belonging, for rethinking the nature of relationships, for the development of reciprocity and mutual pleasure, for re-imagining what it is to be human. Sexuality cannot be separated from gender, but it is not coexistent with it. Indeed, sexuality can be a terrain for the subversion and transgression of gender, and for working through the implications of seeing heterosexuality as just one sexual practice amongst many, not the privileged definer of what is right and wrong (Butler 1993; Segal 1994; Weeks 1995).

4

THE CHALLENGE OF
DIVERSITY

Sexualities keep marching out of the Diagnostic and Statistical Manual
and on to the pages of social history.

Gayle Rubin (1984: 287)

THE LANGUAGE OF PERVERSITY

If the way we think about sex shapes the way we experience it, then
words are tiny marks of those thoughts, haphazard signs scribbled on
the page or floating in the air, which we charge with meaning. Let us
take two words that are common in discussions about sexuality. The first
is 'perversity', the state of being 'perverse' or 'perverted', a turning away
from what is proper and right. The second is 'diversity', the condition
of being 'diverse', concerning 'difference' or 'unlikeness'. The two words
are clearly related, each of them suggesting a move away from a strict
'normality' (another key word). *The Shorter Oxford English Dictionary*
acknowledges the link by recording as one meaning of 'diversity' the word
'perversity', a usage it dates back to the sixteenth century. There is clearly
a common history. Yet when applied to sexuality, the implications
of these words today are distinct. Perversity and diversity may appear

to refer to the same phenomenon. In reality a chasm has opened between them signifying a major shift in the language of sexuality and the way we think about our needs and desires. For while all the terms relating to 'perversity' suggest a hierarchy of sexual values in which 'the perversions' are right at the bottom of the scale, 'diversity' hints at a continuum of behaviours in which one element has no more fundamental a value than any other.

The language of the perverse has always had a strongly moral accent, implying a turning away from what is right, an indulgence in wrong. It is laden with opprobrium. The utilization of terms like perversion and pervert in the sexological writings of the late nineteenth century therefore carried a powerful charge. These terms arose, according to Havelock Ellis (who had himself shown no small skill in deploying them in his earlier writings), at a time when 'sexual anomalies were universally regarded as sins or crimes, at the least as vices' (Ellis 1946: 126). As a result, prohibitions which were rooted in ancient Christian codes were transferred, willy-nilly, to the ostensibly scientific language of the sexological textbooks. Here they became the framework in which clinical investigation of individual sexual lives was conducted, providing definitions, Kinsey sharply commented, nearly identical with 'theologic classifications and with moral pronouncements of the English common law of the fifteenth century' (Kinsey *et al.* 1948: 202). Homosexuality, fetishism, voyeurism, kleptomania, sadism and masochism, transvestism, coprophilia, undinism, frottage, chronic satyriasis and nymphomania, necrophilia, pederasty . . . the list was endless. Each perversion was investigated with dispassionate care and its causes were endlessly speculated upon. Was it a degeneration or a harmless anomaly, congenital or acquired, the result of tainted heredity or the effects of moral corruption, a product of psychic trauma or free and wilful choice? Krafft-Ebing offered a distinction between a *perversion* and a *perversity,* the latter a product of vice, the former a psycho-pathological condition. Havelock Ellis distinguishes between *inversion,* a more or less random biological 'sport', and *perversion*, which sprang from moral indulgence. Magnus Hirschfeld and his followers distinguished *perversions* from *anomalies.* But whatever the speculations about precise demarcations or aetiologies (causes), there was no doubt about the result. Walking out of the pages of these sexological writings, speaking in authentic tones of self-confession (even if their more outrageous memories were carefully censored, accompanied by lines of dots, or rendered in Latin) were real individual beings, marked or marred by their badges of sexual unorthodoxy.

The result of what Foucault has described as the 'perverse implantation' [1] was twofold. On the positive side, the description of these new types of sexual being considerably expanded the definition of what could be considered as 'sexual'. Freud opened his *Three Essays on the Theory of Sexuality* in 1905 with a discussion of homosexuality and other 'sexual aberrations' precisely because he believed that their existence transformed conventional views as to what constituted sex. He used them, as Laplanche and Pontalis put it, 'as a weapon with which to throw the traditional definitions of sexuality into question' (Laplanche and Pontalis 1980: 307). The new definition extended backwards to include even the most modest whispers of infantile sexuality (attachment to the breast, contraction of the bowels, manipulation of the genitals, a generalized sensuality, as well as less overt but more significant Oedipal anxieties) and outwards to the farthest reaches of human behaviour, to embrace not only common or garden variations but also esoteric manifestations that had little obvious connection with orgasm or even pleasure at all. Here were the seeds of a modern view of an infinite sexual variety. But the negative side of this classificatory enthusiasm was a sharp reinforcement of 'the normal'. There was little discussion of heterosexuality as such (there still isn't that much in comparision to our obsession with the 'abnormal'). The term itself emerged, almost reluctantly, *after* homosexuality and originally referred to what we now call bisexuality. Even today it has a vaguely clinical tone to it which limits its common use in everyday speech. But the very absence of speculation about its fundamental nature reinforced its taken-for-granted status, part of the air we breath, the silent assumption which shapes everyday life. Moreover, the debates over the causes of the perversions and the eager descriptions of even their most outrageous examples inevitably worked to emphasize their pathology, their relationship to degeneracy, madness and sickness, and helped to reinforce the normality of heterosexual relations. This served to reinvigorate that disease model of sexuality which enormously influenced twentieth-century ways of thinking about sexual behaviour.

Take, for instance, Freud's attempt to argue for the broadening of the meaning of sexuality. Perversions, he argued in the *Three Essays*, are simply acts which either *extend* sexual practices beyond those regions of the body conventionally designated as appropriate (that is the genitals of either sex), or *linger* over activities that may be proper if they ultimately lead to genital sexuality (the so-called forepleasure, such as kissing, caressing, sucking, biting), but which become perverse if they remain as ends in themselves (Freud 1905). This may be a fair working definitions and it is more generous in its inclusiveness than many others on offer. It is, however, difficult to avoid the conclusion that there is in his mind a model of what sex should be, a goal towards which sexual practices ought to be directed, and hence a prescription of how we must live.

Freud was an interesting example of the ambivalence of these early scientists of sex for the very reason that he went further than anyone else in incorporating the perverse within the acceptable range of sexuality. The effect of the *Three Essays* was to suggest that perversions, far from being the unique property of a sick or immoral minority, are the common property of us all. Their negative was revealed in neurotic symptoms, which were displaced representations of repressed sexual wishes. Their positive presence was demonstrated in forepleasures, and by the social existence of obvious perverts walking the streets, filling the hospitals and the courtrooms. These perversions – 'deviations in respect of sexual object', including homosexuality and bestiality, and 'deviations in respect of sexual aim', whereby pleasure extended beyond genitality – represented the re-emergence of component instincts to which we are all heirs. In the universal polymorphous perversity and bisexuality of infancy Freud was able to find roots of what later sociologists were to label as 'our common deviance':

> No healthy person, it appears, can fail to make some addition that might be called perverse to the normal sexual aim; and the universality of this finding is in itself enough to show how inappropriate it is to use the word perversion as a term of reproach.
>
> (Freud 1905: 160)

But if this is the case, why retain the concept? The attitude of psychoanalysis to homosexuality is revealing here for the very reason that for Freud it was, as he put it, 'scarcely a perversion'. As a result it has become conventional among some contemporary radical defenders of psychoanalysis to remove homosexuality completely from the category of the perverse, while retaining the category itself. But the real interest in Freud's discussion of the topic, in various forms over many years, is his very real ambiguity and reluctance to do this.

On the one hand, Freud carefully examines and rejects conventional sexological views on the subject. He argues that the reduction in the choice of partner to one of the same sex in homosexuality parallels a similar reduction in heterosexuality. As a result, he suggests, 'from the point of view of psycho-analysis the exclusive sexual interest felt by men for women is also a problem that needs elucidating . . . ' (Freud 1905: 146, note 1, added 1915). Homosexuality could not be regarded as a thing apart. In the fact of object choice and genital organization of sexual activity it was often continuous with heterosexuality. Moreover, he wrote in his essay on Leonardo, everyone is capable of homosexual object choice, as the evidence of dreams and fantasies reveals. And homosexual feelings, 'blocked and rechannelled', sublimated into more amorphous emotions of solidarity, brotherhood and sisterhood, were an important element in understanding group psychology. All single-sex institutions, from the sanctity of priestly orders and peace of monasteries and nunneries, to the masculine ethos of military discipline, might in some sense be seen as resting on sublimated homosexuality (Freud 1910: 99, footnote; 1921: 67–143). Freud therefore distanced himself from any idea that homosexuality was a sign of 'degeneracy' – a favoured nineteenth-century term – on the grounds that this was no more than a 'a judgement of value, a condemnation instead of an explanation'. He also rejected the distinction, favoured by Havelock Ellis amongst others, between 'acquired' and 'congenital' homosexuality as being 'fruitless and inappropriate' (Freud 1905: 138–9; 1920: 154). Homosexuality, like its sibling form heterosexuality, can only be understood in relation to the working of the psychic apparatus as a whole. Its roots were to be found in the universal bisexuality to which we are born, and in the mental processes by which each individual negotiated the hazards of castration anxiety and the Oedipus crisis to obtain a precarious 'sexual identity'.

So, homosexuality was not a disease. It needed no 'cure'. It was widespread. It was continuous with heterosexuality in many of its forms. And like this, it was not a single condition, but more a grouping of different activities, needs and desires:

> What we have thrown together, for reasons of convenience, under the name of homosexuality, may derive from a diversity of processes of psycho-social inhibitions.
>
> (Freud 1905: 146)

Here, apparently, once and for all, we see homosexuality demystified. No longer need it be hidden under a stone like worms and other disturbing creatures. It was a more or less ordinary phenomenon, part of the life of us all, and now subjected to the light of scientific reason. And yet, and yet . . . that is not quite how it has been seen within psychoanalysis, nor was it in practice how ultimately Freud himself was able to leave the subject. The problem is encapsulated in the word 'inhibition'. For while on the one hand we have this rational deconstruction of homosexuality, on the other we are offered a model of sexuality which assumes a normal pattern of development, and which therefore makes homosexuality highly problematic as a life choice. In his famous letter to the mother of a young homosexual, Freud assured her that homosexuality was no vice or degradation, nor was it an illness: it was nothing to be ashamed of. But, he added: 'We consider it to be a variation of the sexual function produced by a certain arrest of the sexual development' (E. Freud 1961: 277). Therein lies the difficulty. A 'development' assumes an appropriate end result, and 'arrest' an artificial blockage. For Freud the growth of each individual from infancy to mature adult sexuality repeated the (hypothetical) development of the race as a whole from primitive sexual promiscuity and perversity to monogamous heterosexuality. This was not a product simply of evolution but of cultural imperatives. It was the tragic destiny of humankind necessarily to forgo the infinite range of the desires in order to ensure survival in a world of scarcity. Each individual, like the race itself, had to attain the 'tyranny of genital organisation' in order to survive, while appropriate object choice became less an act of volition and more a cultural demand. In the end, therefore, a heterosexual and reproductive imperative is reinserted into Freud's account. Once a goal-directed version of sexuality is introduced, however surreptitiously, then the whole laboriously constructed edifice of sexual variety begins to totter.

For Freud, the term 'perversion' had a precise technical meaning, as an aspect of all our lives we could not escape. It was a problem only when it became an end in itself and blocked the road to 'mature sexuality'.

But it was very difficult to separate that meaning from the wider moral and political meanings attached to it. A crack was left in the door which allowed judgemental values to re-enter a supposedly neutral clinical discourse. Many post-Freudians eagerly pushed the door wide open.

So, for example, Ernest Jones, one of Freud's most loyal supporters and his biographer, criticized him for an over-tolerant attitude to his lesbian patient and commented that 'much is gained if the path to heterosexual gratification is opened . . . ' (Jones 1955: 299). Later Freudians, in their haste to abandon the idea that homosexuality itself was not a pathology, have even junked Freud's central concept of universal bisexuality. For Socarides, heterosexuality was the natural state from which homosexuality was a deviation. He observes that one of the curious resistances of his patients lay in their assumption that their disorder was 'a normal form of sexuality', and suggests that 'these views must be dealt with from the very beginning' (Socarides 1978). For Elizabeth Moberly, 'heterosexuality is the goal of human development . . . ' (Moberly 1983). In such comments we can see a return to a pre-Freudian moralism. Freud himself can scarcely be blamed for this. Nevertheless the seeds of such positions are sown by the ambiguities of Freud's own writings. He speaks, at various times, of homosexuality as an abnormality, a disorder, as pathological, and in the male case a 'flight from women'. Indeed, occasionally he even described it without ambiguity as 'a perversion'. Nor is this ultimately surprising. In the last resort, whatever the qualifications in the statement that the germ of perversion is present in us all, the notion of development must imply a norm.

The founders of sexology – and here Freud, one of its most radical figures, was no exception – constructed a unitary model of sexuality from which it has been difficult to escape. On the one hand, we were offered a norm of behaviour, which was heterosexual, procreative and largely male, in which female sexuality has almost invariably been defined as secondary or responsive to the male's. (This applied, it must be added, even to the concept of perversion itself. As Plummer has put it, the field of sexual deviation has mainly been demarcated by the issue of male desire (Plummer 1984: 219). Female breaches with the norm were fitted into a dichotomized picture of male activity and female passivity. Not surprisingly, the most commonly recognized female sexual deviations include servicing men in prostitution or pornography, or 'provoking' men, as in accounts of rape; and lesbianism, the most common form of female sexual variation, has generally been speculated about in terms which derived entirely from the male.) On the other hand, there was an ever-growing catalogue of perversions, deviations, paraphilias, call them what you will, which inevitably marginalized and in the last resort pathologized other sexualities. The language of perversion divided the sexual world into the normal and the abnormal, the elect and the damned, and rarely did they meet.

THE DISCOURSE OF DIVERSITY

A 'perverse dynamic', Dollimore has argued, lies at the heart of western constructions of sexuality (Dollimore 1991). The striving to produce and regulate the norm inevitably produces the Other, the feared and execrated or merely despised, which simultaneously denies and confirms the norm. The political and sexual ordering is always internally dis-ordered by the very perversities it produces and sets up against itself. That disorder, of course, provides the elements of resistance, subversion and transgression, and ultimately the notion of a pluralism of sexualities, of diversity as a fact of life. In two critical areas, one theoretical, the other political, a 'discourse of diversity' has arisen, and it has had significant cultural effects.

The first area is that of sexology itself. On one level it is little more than a cosmetic terminological change, signalled as early as the 1930s by Havelock Ellis himself. The term 'perversion', he suggested, 'is com-pletely antiquated and mischievous and should be avoided' (Ellis 1946: 127). He offered as a replacement the less fevered (if still ideologically laden) term, 'sexual deviation', and this phrase became commonplace in sociological discussions in the half century or so afterwards. Latent in such shifts of terminology was a more important change: the recognition of sexual pluralism and the emergence of what Gayle Rubin has described as the concept of a 'benign sexual variation' (Rubin 1984).

The seeds of this new approach were clearly planted by the investigations of the founding sexologists themselves, and the delicate plants were nourished by an appropriation of the Freudian advocacy of a common infantile polymorphous perversity. The celebration of desire as many-sided and many-shaped by some modern writers has taken this position to its logical, often morally anarchic, conclusion. The key figure in transforming the public debate, apart from Freud, was Kinsey. Coming close, as he rather reluctantly admitted, to Freud's speculations, he suggested that there was an important idea that rarely featured prominently in either general or scientific discussion, that sex was a normal biological function, acceptable in whatever form it appeared: he wrote to a boy struggling with homosexual feelings, 'Biologically there is no form of outlet which I will admit as abnormal. There is no right or wrong biologically' (Pomeroy 1972). Such statements were clearly still in the naturalistic framework of the sexual tradition and in that form must be taken with a pinch of scepticism. Their echoes are more likely to be found today in the speculations of those sociobiologists and others who profess to see a genetic functionalism in sexual variations than in the writings of sociologists or historians. Yet the underlying message has become crucial to contemporary debates. Few sexologists in the mainstream would feel relaxed at using a term like 'perversion' to describe the varieties of sexual patterns today. For one of the most influential studies on the subject, by Robert Stoller, perversion is 'the erotic form of hatred', defined not so much by the acts *(the* perversions) but by the content, hostility, while the term 'pervert' for describing a particular type of person is banned completely from sexological debates. There is even a new and welcome modesty abroad, admitting that ' . . . it is crucial to remember that we still know very little about the mechanisms or causes of human sexual behaviour . . . ' (Stoller 1977: 45). Such modesty works against categorical positions.

But if we know little about the causes, we do know increasingly about the forms and frequent occurrence of sexual diversity, and this rather than his questionable biologism is Kinsey's real contribution. The two vast volumes he largely wrote, *Sexual Behavior in the Human Male* and *Sexual Behavior in the Human Female,* and the others he inspired, may have had methodological problems and insufficiently representative samples, and are suffused with unconscious biases of their own. But the thousands of subjects he and his colleagues interviewed provided an unparalleled insight into American sexual life. When it became possible to say, on the basis of what was then the most thorough investigation ever done, that 37 per cent of the male sample had had sexual contact to orgasm with another male, then even if the sample was unrepresentative and the percentage figures were exaggerated, homosexual activity could no longer be seen as a morbid symptom of a tiny, sick minority. At least amongst a significant section of American life it was a fairly common occurrence. And if this was true of homosexuality, then it was potentially true also for a wide range of other sexualities, from bestiality to paedophilia, from sado-masochism to a passion for pornography. Kinsey was fascinated by the range of variations in human sexual behaviours. He cited with glee the example of two men who lived in the same town, met at the same place of business, had common social activities, and yet experienced enormously different sexual lives. One individual he interviewed had had one ejaculation in thirty years; another had thirty a week, a difference of 45,000 times. This was just one example for Kinsey of the vast variety that existed, across the divide of class, gender and race. From this flowed a profoundly important and influential sociological – and political – point. He wrote:

> The publicly pretended code of morals, our social organization, our marriage customs, our sex laws, and our educational and religious systems are based upon an assumption that individuals are much alike sexually and that it is an equally simple matter for all of them to confine their behavior to the single pattern which the mores dictate.
>
> (Kinsey *et al.* 1948: 197)

But what if people were in fact different, had different needs, desires and behaviour? Then a yawning gap would appear between moral codes and sexual behaviour, throwing into confusion the absolutist certainties of the sexual tradition. This was the favoured point of departure for subsequent critiques of normative regulations.

If transformations within mainstream sexology provided a theoretical framework for a recognition of diversity, the political energy came from a different source, that of the 'sexual minorities' themselves. We noted earlier that since at least the nineteenth century most industrial societies have witnessed a sustained effort to articulate and develop distinct lesbian and male homosexual identities in the context of extending subcultures and social communities. As the homosexual ways of life have become more public and self-confident, so in their wake other assertions of minority sexual identities have emerged. The example of homosexuality, as Gayle Rubin has argued, has provided a repertoire of political strategies and organizational forms for the mobilization of other erotic populations (Rubin 1984). Transvestites, transsexuals, paedophiles, sado-masochists, fetishists, bisexuals, prostitutes/sex workers and others vocally emerged, clamouring for their right of self-expression and legitimacy, with varying degrees of successful recognition. The hesitantly speaking perverts of Krafft-Ebing's medico-forensic pages, confessing their most intimate secrets to the new sexual experts, have walked out of the clinical text and onto the stage of history, the living proof of sexual diversity.

These new sexual and social identities may have emerged on the terrain first mapped and carefully articulated by the sexologists themselves. But as Kinsey himself forcefully observed, it is only the human mind which invents categories and tries to force facts into separate pigeonholes; and the facts constantly subvert.

Sexology was important in establishing the language by which these miscreants were described and analysed. Through their symbiotic relationship with the medical profession (many of them, like Ellis and Hirschfeld, were trained doctors, though other influential figures were not) these early sexologists helped construct a very influential disease model, the effects of which are still with us. But the poor creatures they described were not their inventions: they were products of very complex social processes, of social definition and of self-definition in which sexology played an important but not decisive part. Moreover, the language of sexology could itself be used to challenge the certainties of the sexual tradition.

I started this chapter with words. Several other words symbolize the movement both of language and everyday life (as far as they can be distinguished): 'sodomite', 'homosexual', 'gay', 'queer'. Just as the widespread emergence (at first in America) of the self-description 'gay' in the 1950s and 1960s marked a crucial new stage in the growth of a politicized sexual identity based around same-sex desires, the gradual spread of the term 'homosexual' from the late nineteenth century marked a significant breach with the traditional terminology of the sin that could not be named amongst Christians, that of sodomy. 'Sodomite' was a term suffused with heavy tones of mediaeval morality. It was also ambiguous. It signified someone who committed a particular type of sexual *act*, that of buggery or anal intercourse. The homosexual, on the other hand, was a particular type of sexual *person*, given not only a name but a personalized history (weak father, strong mother, or sometimes overbearing father and submissive mother), physical characteristics (wide hips and high voice if a man, masculinized figure and hair on the upper lip if a woman), and indicative failures (inability to whistle, dislike of children). Many thus described by the clinical discourse might not recognize themselves fully or at all in such descriptions; but they were able to validate their existence, affirm that others like them existed by their naming, and that, far from being unique creatures, they could re-enter the canons of recognized, if perverted, sexualities. A new language of self-description emerged – 'invert', 'uranian', 'third' or 'intermediate' sex – that marked the embryonic stirring of an affirmative, and modern, sense of self.

The universal adoption of the term 'gay' in all Anglophone countries from the early 1970s can be seen as a new stage in the public expression of a positive personal identity, by creating a clear *social* identity organized around sexuality. The search for valid sexual identities has characterized the history of homosexuality, male and female, since the nineteenth century. Different groups of people have found different ways of doing this: there is no pre-ordained goal. Gender, geographical and racial differences have produced differentiated identities. Many make no connection whatsoever between their sexual practices and their social identity. But for many establishing a firm sense of sexual identity remained essential. Categorization and self-labellings, that is the process of working out a social identity, may control, restrict and inhibit, as many critics have argued, but at the same time they provide, as Plummer has noted, 'comfort, security and assuredness' (Plummer 1980: 29). And a precondition for attaining a secure sense of personal identity and belonging has been the development of wider social networks, of finding a collective way of dealing with sexual differentiation, of establishing sexual communities and social worlds, of telling their stories in ways which could make for mutual recognition and support.

The emergence of distinctive sexual subcultures and communities is part of a wider process that has marked the modern world, and is becoming ever more characteristic of the era of late or post-modernity, that of ever-growing social complexity and social differentiation, producing a new pluralism of class, ethnic, racial and cultural forms as well as a diversity of gender and sexual experiences. This process of differentiation has of course produced not only complexity but new forms of social conflict and antagonism. It is in the context of continuing struggle over appropriate behaviour that politicized sexual identities also emerged, articulated since the late nineteenth century (hesitantly at first) in a series of homosexual rights groupings and other sex reform movements throughout the industrialized world. These have been an important way of sexual outsiders responding to the changing patterns of sexual regulation and of challenging sexual norms.

Sociologists have suggested a number of factors that are necessary for this successful emergence: the existence of large numbers in the same situation; geographical concentration; identifiable targets of opposition; sudden events or changes in social position; and an intellectual leadership with readily understood goals (Adam 1978, 1995; D'Emilo 1983). Each of these was present in the history of homosexual movements at various times, which explains its significant social presence compared to other sexual minorities. Already by the late nineteenth century there were large numbers of men who saw themselves as 'homosexual', emerging from and increasingly constructing subcultures and their own social worlds. Lesbian groupings were more embryonic; nevertheless, in many North American and European cities both an identity and social networks were developing. These were the seedbeds of support for such organizations as Magnus Hirschfeld's Scientific-Humanitarian Committee in Germany, founded in 1898, and the smaller sex reform organizations in Britain and elsewhere, founded on the eve of the First World War. The organizations fluctuated in their fortunes as political circumstances changed. The German homosexual movement, at one time the largest in the world, was effectively destroyed by the Nazis during the 1930s. By the 1950s nevertheless there was a new initiative, this time based in the United States of America. Organizations like the Mattachine society and the Daughters of Bilitis were founded partly in the wake of the McCarthyite witch hunts against sexual deviants in the early 1950s, but also in the context of expanding subcultures of male homosexuals and lesbians during the post-war decade. It was the juncture of the increasingly sophisticated gay communities of cities like New York and San Francisco with a newly politicized movement of 'gay liberationists' in the late 1960s that provided the energy for the emergence of mass gay and lesbian movements in the USA in the 1970s and 1980s. This provided a model which other countries followed wherever local conditions permitted.

Conditions that made it possible for homosexuality to find a voice have not always been present for other groupings. The intense stigma attached to inter-generational sex, and its inevitable overlap with child sex abuse has made it very difficult for its advocates to develop a substantial subculture, find a common voice or group together over long periods in stable organizations. Characteristic organizations that developed in the 1970s, like NAMBLA (North America Man Boy Love Association) in the United States and PIE (Paedophile Information Exchange) in Britain, soon experienced social obloquy and constant police attention even for advocating changed attitudes. Perhaps more crucially, it is not an activity that lends itself easily to the establishment of stable social communities (whatever the public perception of conspiracies of abusers), given the social hostility and the transient nature of many paedophile relations, stemming from the fact that children tend to grow up, and the disparity in interest between adults and children. Advocates of sado-masochistic sexual activity (SM) are also likely to be limited in number, which inhibits the establishment of large-scale movements, though they have developed support networks and subcultures in various cities across the globe. SM also became an issue of major sexual political controversy in various radical movements, with both the feminist and gay and lesbian movements sharply divided about the merits of such activities. Issues related to transgendered activities (cross-dressing and transsexuality) have also split these movement, though controversies in these cases have not been so much about sexual activity as about their claimed perpetuation of existing gender stereotypes. Prostitutes and other sex workers (in pornography, strip clubs, etc.) have posed different problems again for political organization: about the validity of working in the commercial sexual field and about women servicing male fantasies, which often involve the playing out of desires for violence and degradation.

But although the conditions for the emergence of powerful political organizations on the model of gay and lesbian groupings may vary, the fact is that through an increasingly globalized world new communities have emerged around sexual issues, and through these a range of sexual identities have been affirmed. There no longer appears to be a great continent of normality surrounded by small islands of disorder. Instead we can now witness huge clusters of islands, great and small, which seem in constant motion one to the other, each with its own unique vegetation and geography. New categories and erotic minorities have emerged. Older ones have experienced a process of subdivision as specialized tastes, specific aptitudes and needs become the basis for proliferating sexual identities. The list is potentially endless as each specific desire becomes a locus of political statement and possible social identity.

A number of questions inevitably arise: is each form of desire of equal validity? Should each subdivision of desire be the basis of a sexual and possible social identity? Is each claim for identity of equal weight in the debates of sexual politics? What about the heterosexual identity, which is rarely articulated but provides the master discourse? Is identity indeed an appropriate category for thinking of the flux of erotic experience? Does identity not delimit, constrict and constrain free choice? Aren't identities simply narrative devices to provide a sense of security and stability, ultimately fictions, if 'necessary fictions' (Plummer 1995; Weeks 1995)? And what about the language of sexuality? Earlier I signalled that the term 'queer' is part of this complex history of sexual identity. For decades a term signalling both external opprobrium and subcultural self-description in the world of homosexuality, the gay liberationists decisively abandoned it in the 1970s because of its connotations of self-loathing. By the 1990s, however, it had been adopted again by sex radicals, as a mark of rejection of the idea of fixed identities, and as a challenge to the heteronormative structuring of sexuality (Warner 1993). The perverse, far from being a signifier of sickness, was a position from which the norm could be challenged. Transgression becomes the defining characteristic of a politics of subversion. Identity, it seems, is not enough.

But that still leaves, hovering gently but firmly over our heads, the most difficult but decisive question of all. If we reject, as I believe we must, the traditional concept of the perverse altogether in favour of a discourse of diversity, are there any means by which we can distinguish the good from the bad, the appropriate from the inappropriate and, dare we say it, the moral from the immoral? To affirm the existence of diversity does not answer difficult questions posed by the sexual tradition: it merely raises new ones.

DECONSTRUCTING THE CATEGORIES

The first point to make is that the admitted fact of sexual diversity need not lead to a norm of diversity. The efforts made by social moralists and fundamentalist groupings to encourage or enforce a return to 'traditional values' suggests that some people at least have not given up the hope of a revival of a universal moral standard. There are powerful tendencies amongst quite disparate groups to search for a 'new morality' in which the corrupt elements of a liberal/capitalist/bourgeois/Western/ male-dominated/heterosexist society – the language varies – could be finally eliminated. The problem here lies in the fact that even amongst the sexually marginalized and vocal sexual minorities there is often little agreement, indeed sometimes there is violent disagreement. Is pornography constitutive of male violence, or a reflection of a generally sexist society, or harmless? Is inter-generational sex a radical challenge to arbitrary divisions of age, or is it child sex abuse? Is transgendered behaviour a challenge to the tyranny of gender stereotypes or is it a surrender to such sexual divisions and stereotypes? Does sado-masochism involve a submersion in dangerous fantasies – or worse – of violence, or is it no more than a harmless playing out of eroticized power relations? These questions and many others are important, because they challenge us to rethink the criteria by which we are able to decide between appropriate and inappropriate behaviour.

The sexual tradition for a long time basically offered only two positions: either sex is fundamentally dangerous, acceptable only when channelled into appropriate channels (generally, marital procreative sex); or sex is basically healthy and good, but it has been repressed, distorted and denied by a corrupt society. There is a third approach, which is the one I have advocated in this essay: that sex only attains meaning in social relations, which implies that we can only make appropriate choices around sexuality by understanding its social, cultural and political context. This involves a decisive move away from the morality of 'acts' , which has dominated sexual theorizing for hundreds of years, and in the direction of a new relational perspective which takes into account context and meanings [2]. Many still take it for granted that sin or salvation, morality or immorality, normality or abnormality reside in what we do. This was enshrined in the Christian codes of the Middle Ages, in the tables that declared that heterosexual rape was higher up the scale of value than masturbation or consensual sodomy, because the former was procreative and the latter were barren. There, the priority given to reproduction dictated the hierarchy of value.

In the twenty-first century we are ostensibly more tolerant (though that is not always apparent in those fundamentalist regimes which believe that homosexuals or female adulterers deserve being stoned to death in the name of religious values), but many still take for granted the assumption that some practices are inherently better than others. Now, however, we tend to give more credit to nature, biology, or the science of sex rather than blind faith for revealing this hierarchy. Anal intercourse is no longer the worst crime known to Christians – though it is still illegal in some parts of the USA. Masturbation is no longer the gateway to horrors amongst young people, and is encouraged by books, magazines and papers on every station bookstall, and one of the pleasures incited by the internet. Sometimes this escalator effect is because of scientific reassessment. More usually it is the result of moral and political changes helped by well-organized campaigns. It was the militant organization of homosexuals, not any scientific breakthrough, that led to the removal of homosexuality from the list of diseases of the American Psychiatric Association in 1974 [3]. Passionate campaigns by feminists, social purity men and women, and reformers of various persuasions over the past hundred years, not advances in knowledge, have shifted perceptions of sexual abuse, pornography and prostitution, birth control and abortion in various directions. But the unconscious belief that some acts are better than others still exists, even if, in a pluralistic world, we cannot always agree what that order ought to be.

A relational perspective attempts, on the other hand, to understand all these sexual practices as aspects of wider social relations, to unravel the context in which acts become meaningful. This in turn involves attempting to understand the power relations at play, the subtle coercions which limit the possibilities of choice, the likely impact of a particular sexual activity on the self and others, as well as the possibilities of pleasure and personal autonomy that may be encouraged. There are very difficult issues at stake in such an endorsement of moral pluralism, and I shall attempt to explore these later. The point that needs underlining here is that such a perspective must involve breaking with any moral system based on acts as such.

There is, however, perhaps an even more challenging implication. In the sexual tradition certain acts have been seen as living examples of a particular sexual system, manifestations of a syndrome. The perspective outlined here breaks with such unitary categories. If we do this it will no longer be possible to condemn a sexual practice because it is 'homosexual' or 'heterosexual', 'sado-masochistic' or even 'paedophile'. Instead we should begin to ask: what makes this particular activity valid or invalid, appropriate or inappropriate? What are the social factors that make these meaningful? What are the power relations at work?

If we take three examples we will see the type of factors that must be taken into account. The first example is of heterosexuality. At first sight this may seem surprising. Heterosexuality is so much taken for granted as the norm that it is rarely questioned. It is the given of sexual theorizing, the natural form by which we judge others. Until quite recently, there has been little attempt to theorize it, or trace its history (Katz 1995). Some feminist critics of its current form have ended up by rejecting all forms of heterosexuality because it supposedly perpetuates male dominance. For writers such as Adrienne Rich, as we have seen, 'compulsory heterosexuality' is the key mechanism of control of women, and hence institutionalized heterosexuality is the master discourse that shapes and defines the sexual order (Rich 1984; see also Jackson 2000).

But whilst recognizing the power of the institutionalized form, we also need to be aware of different contexts and meanings. Heterosexuality may well be an institution but it is also a series of practices, not a single phenomenon. The term embraces loving relationships as well as rape, choice as well as coercion. It covers a multitude of sexual activities from intercourse in the missionary position to oral and anal intercourse. As a term it obscures differences of age, of gender, of culture and even of the fantasies of the partners involved. A relational perspective would start out not with the object choice or the act (genital intercourse) which is taken as its most characteristic form, but with the host of factors that shape its significance. Is the sexual act itself one means of perpetuating relations of domination and subordination? If so, what are the alternatives? Does the possibility exist for equal relations between the man and woman? Is change necessary, desirable, possible? Such are the questions posed by a rethinking of heterosexuality [4].

The power relations that sex can involve are most dramatically illustrated by the question of sex between the generations, or paedophilia. Few topics arouse such fear and anxiety in contemporary societies. The 'paedophile' has become a symbol of predatory evil, a synonym indeed not only for child abuser but also in many cases for child abductor and even murderer. The peculiar horror invoked by the abuse of innocence, by the imposition of adult desires on the vulnerable, powerless child, speaks for a culture that is sensitive to the differences between adults and children, and is concerned with protecting the young as long as possible. Yet this has not always been the case. In the late nineteenth century paedophilia was lauded by some for its pedagogic possibilities – the so-called Greek love justification: in the passage from childhood dependence to adult responsibility, guidance, sexual and moral, of a caring man can be invaluable, it was argued. It was further legitimated in the twentieth century by the supposed facts of childhood sexuality: sexology itself has revealed the wide extent of childhood sexual potentiality including the existence of infantile masturbation. If something is so natural, and omnipresent, should it be as rigidly controlled as childhood sexuality is today? And again, if it is natural, then surely it cannot be harmful even if it takes place with adults. As Tom O'Carroll, a militant supporter of inter-generational sex (who ended up in prison for his pains) wrote '. . . there is no need whatever for a child to know "the consequences" of engaging in harmless sex play, simply because it is exactly that: harmless' [5].

For the vast majority of the population this is not harmless play, it is simply child sex abuse. It involves powerful adults using their experience and wiles to gain satisfaction from exploiting children. The growing sensitivity to abuse is the result of long campaigns, often led in Western countries by feminists, or by campaigners who experienced abuse themselves. This has become a global phenomenon, with international campaigns to end the traffic in children and the worst abuses of sex tourism. This without doubt marks an advance in society's awareness of the reality of exploitation, and the power of adults over children. Yet there is something rather odd in the ways in which various late modern societies, from Australia to Europe to the USA, have focused on the figure of the anonymous paedophile rather than on the hard reality that most abuse of children is carried out by a close relative or family friend, or perhaps by a priest, as a wave of scandals from the UK and Ireland to Australia and the USA has recently underscored [6].

Despite, or perhaps because of, the emotiveness of the issue, it is important to be as rational as possible in looking at what is involved. Age is an ambiguous marker. Is there an ideal age at which consent becomes free, rather than abusive, and a relationship becomes consensual, rather than coercive? Certainly the vast majority of us could agree that it should not be 3 or 8, but what about 12 or 14 or 15 which are the ages of consent in various European countries? Laws vary enormously, and sometimes affect boys and girls quite differently. Brian Taylor has pointed to the existence of eight possible subcategories of inter-generational sex, depending on the age of those involved, the distinction of gender, the nature of the sexual proclivity, and the interaction of all three (Taylor 1981). This suggests that there are paedophilias, not a single paedophilia, and the social response should be sensitive to these distinctions, even as it focuses rightly on protecting the young and vulnerable.

Power is an acute issue in discussions of inter-generational sex. In consensual sado-masochism this is taken a step further, to the eroticization of power itself. As an early advocate of consensual SM put it: 'we select the most frightening, disgusting or unacceptable activities and transmute them into pleasure' (Califia 1979: 19). For the theorists of the sexual tradition, SM had its roots in an exaggeration of the normal relations intrinsic between men and women. For Krafft-Ebing, sadism was 'nothing else than excessive and monstrous pathological intensifi-cation of phenomena – possible too in normal conditions, in rudimental forms – which accompany the psychical sexual life, particularly in males . . . Masochism is the opposite of sadism . . .' (Weinberg and Levi Kamel 1983: 27). Yet for many advocates of SM from within the sexual subcultures of the West, it provides unique insights into the nature of sexual power, therapeutic and cathartic sex revealing the nature of sex as ritual and play [7]. Such claims are no doubt exaggerated, but what they effectively do is pose very dramatically the question of the relationship between context and choice, subjectivity and consent in thinking about sexuality. Should people have the right to consent to activities that are conventionally regarded as painful and potentially harmful? What are the conditions that make such choices valid? Is there the same possibility of free choice between say a man and a woman as there is between people of 'the same caste' (gay, two women)? The activities of the 'sexual fringe', of which SMers are among the most radically transgressive members, may remain marginal to the mainstream of most people's sexual lives, but they do in fact ask major questions about what are the limits of normality, what are the boundaries of valid sexual activity, and what are the extremes to which we should go in the pursuit of pleasure.

At the end of the nineteenth century, when these issues began to be aired in the discreet pages of the new sexology, the appetite for knowledge may have been substantial, but the audience was relatively limited.

Today, we live in the midst of a discursive explosion, a vast efflorescence of sexual stories (Plummer 1995). Some individuals may be too shy or modest to confess their secret desires to their partners or closest friends but appear to have no difficulty in telling all to millions of television viewers, or in indulging their fantasies across the anonymous spaces of the internet. We have come a long way. But the fact that we can tell our stories so insistently does not obviate the fact that stories have different weightings, embody diverse values, and impact differentially on people. We still need to make distinctions. A disaggregation of sexual practices along the lines I propose here opens them up to social and political interrogation. Inevitably we will not find simple answers for and against particular activities in doing this. But deconstructing the unitary categories of the moralists and the early sexologists has the inestimable value of opening up crucial debates about the parameters within which valid decisions and choices can be made.

Two final points need to be made. First of all, the acceptance of the idea that there are benign social variations must not imply an abandonment of distinctions. There are certain classes of act connected with sex that can find universal condemnation as malignant, especially those involving deliberate acts of violence, whether in the form of sexual murder, rape, or child abuse. This is the class that Stoller appears to be addressing in his attempt to theorize perversion as the erotic form of hatred. It is a potentiality in all of us, in his view, which relates to the tensions and anxieties produced by the necessity of attaining particular gender identities. There may well be scope for the development of theoretical insights into the nature of aberrant activities in this way – though that is a question that needs to be left to another place, another time. The issue that needs stressing is that, even here, it is not the act itself which constitutes the problem but the whole context – social and psychic – that gives rise to it, and from which it takes its meaning; factors such as family circumstances or male anxiety and power. In other words, if the perversion in this sophisticated psychoanalytic approach is in fact a revolt against the limits imposed by culture, a means of eluding, in Chasseguet-Smirgel's phrase, 'the fatal character of the Oedipus complex', a life-denying leap away from reality, then it is still that culture, that reality which can help us to understand the individual activity (Chasseguet-Smirgel 1985: 26). The traditional concentration on the aetiology of the individual's act can no longer be sufficient.

This leads to the second point, concerning the real meaning of the concept of diversity. As Plummer has said:

> however neutral and objective talk about sexual diversity appears to be, it is also talk about *power*. Every culture has to establish – through both formal and informal political processes-the range and scope of the diversities that will be outlawed or banned. No culture could function with a sexual free-for-all, but the pattern of these constraints is exceedingly variable across time and space.
>
> (Plummer 1984: 219)

The vital point here is that the distinctions we make are in the last resort ethical or political ones, dependent less on the rational weighing of evidence than on the political balance of forces. It is for this reason that questions of sexuality are inevitably, inescapably, political questions. What is ultimately wrong with the traditional use of the term 'perversion' is that its ostensibly scientific terminology obscures moral and political judgements. It forecloses discussion. The advantage of embracing the term 'diversity' is that it leaves the important questions wide open – to debate, negotiation, and political choice.

5

SEXUALITY, INTIMACY AND POLITICS

> . . . there is no aspect of human behaviour about which there has been
> more thought, more talk, and more books written.
>
> Alfred Kinsey *et al.* (1948: 21)

SEXUALITY: ON THE FRONT LINE OF POLITICS

Concern with sexuality has been at the heart of Western preoccupations
since before the triumph of Christianity. It has been a matter of political debate for something like two hundred years. Already, by the last
decades of the nineteenth century, the preoccupations of second-wave
feminism were on the agenda: concerning male power over women, sexual
exploitation, the differences between men and women and the meaning
of consent and choice. By the 1920s and 1930s, with the rise and fall
of a world sex reform movement, and the apparently irresistible rise and
rise of social authoritarianism and fascism, the intricate connections
between sexual values and political power were clearly visible. It was
during this period, through the writings of such people as Wilhelm
Reich, that a concept connecting sex and politics – 'sexual politics' – first
came into being.

It is fair to say, nevertheless, that only since the 1960s has the idea of sexual politics had any real impact and resonance, moving from the periphery to the centre in terms of policy, and moving from the original heartlands of modernity to the rest of the globe in terms of geo-political resonance. Today we take the centrality of sexuality for granted as a powerful contemporary reality: the phrase 'sexual politics' has become almost a cliché, yet its ramifications run through the whole of contemporary social life and politics. Moreover, it is no longer a politics confined to what can broadly be called 'the left' or 'progressive' circles. Since the 1970s and early 1980s some of the most skilful and influential developments of a politics around sexuality have come from conservative forces, whether the moral traditionalists of western cultures, or the 'fundamentalists' of Christianity, Islam, Hinduism or Judaism across the globe. To an unexpected and unusual degree, sexuality has become a battleground for contending political forces, a front-line of contemporary politics. It seems that for many the struggle for the future of society must be fought on the terrain of contemporary sexuality. As sexuality goes, so goes society. But equally, as society goes, so goes sexuality (Weeks 1995).

This intense preoccupation with the erotic simultaneously grows out of, and contributes to what Anthony Giddens has described as a 'transformation of intimacy' (Giddens 1992). At its centre is a critical, if as we have seen so far unfinished, revolution in the relations between men and women, profoundly unsettled by rapid social change and by the rise of modern feminism, with its wide-ranging critiques of, and challenges to, the various forms of male domination and female subordination. This is the meaning of the politics of sexuality in its broadest sense: a struggle over the present and future of sexual difference and gender division, a struggle which has at its heart the aspiration towards egalitarian relations and social justice. But this in turn feeds a growing crisis over the broader meaning of sexuality in our culture, about the place we give to the erotic in our lives and relationships, about identity and pleasure, obligation and power, choice and consent. The fixed points which seemed to organize and regulate our sexual beliefs and morals – religious, familial, heterosexual, monogamous – have been radically undermined during the past century. And far from abating, the rate of change is gathering speed as the forces of globalization ensure that no sexual culture can escape the challenge of 'detraditionalization'. The rule of 'traditional values' may have been partial and ineffective; the norms may have been restrictive and authoritarian. But the apparent eclipse of their hegemony has left a vacuum. We are no longer quite sure – or at least agreed on – what we mean by sexuality, or what its role in social and individual lives should be.

Increasing numbers of people no longer look to tradition to find their moral and ethical anchors. They are forced by the juggenaut of change to find their lodestars in themselves, in their individual judgement and choices. This can be liberating; it can also face individuals with the loneliness, the terror, of moral choice. This new individualism in turn is part of the ever-growing complexity of late modern societies. There is a new pluralism of beliefs and behaviours abroad, going beyond a diversity of sexual activities to a wide range of patterns of relationships reflecting generational, cultural, ethnic, communal and political difference. Perhaps this pluralism was always there, beneath our unsuspecting, moralistic eyes: there is growing historical, anthropological and sociological evidence to suggest this. Under the uniformity propounded by religious or national traditions there always lay the devil of diversity. Nevertheless, the recognition of sexual and social diversity as a spectacular fact of the contemporary, increasingly globalized, world, has sharpened the dilemma of how to cope with it in social policy and personal practice. It is this that explains the sexualization of the political agenda in many diverse societies: a growing prioritization of those issues which have been shaping and reshaping moral debates for well over a hundred years, but whose profile has been frequently obscured or marginalized in mainstream politics until the transformations that are making and remaking our confused, complex, turbulent and ever-shifting present.

Rapid change breeds a profound nostalgia, a melancholic longing for the pieties and simplicities of a lost era. It seems to be one of the characteristics of people faced by social change to yearn for a return to a supposed 'golden age' of order, decency, discipline and propriety. The difficulty is that the more we search for it, the more we seem to find ourselves locked into an endless maze where the goal is always just around the next corner. Traditionalists in many Western countries have ventured various historical possibilities. Was this 'golden age' in the 1950s, before the supposed descent into 'permissiveness' during the 1960s, with what the former British prime minister Margaret Thatcher called its denigration of 'the old virtues of discipline and self-restraint'

[1]? Or could it be found in the years between the great world wars, when writers like the pioneering British advocate of birth control, Marie Stopes, looked forward to a 'glorious unfolding' in relations between men and women? Or perhaps we may find traces of it in the last great flowering of peace and social hierarchy before the outbreak of the First World War, if we ignore its materialist excesses and upper-class philanderings? Each of these periods has had its advocates as a 'golden age' – but, more important, each also had its own prophets of decline and doom, looking yet further back. Yet they of course have an air of provincialism when put into the world-historic certainties and grand perspectives of eternity offered by the fundamentalist prophets, who see modernity itself as the enemy (even as they exploit its scientific breakthroughs to create transnational movements for moral regeneration) (Bhatt 1997).

The historical accuracy of a reference point in the past is, of course, irrelevant to its contemporary power. It provides a yardstick with which to judge the present, usually revealing more about our current discontents than past realities. More particularly, the glorification of the past enables people in the present to pinpoint the imagined movement of decline. The British conservative journalist, Ronald Butt, spoke for many moral traditionalists and theorists of cultural decline when he described the triumph of a new liberalism in the 1960s. Its essence, he wrote, was:

> permissiveness in one strictly limited social area (i.e. sex) coupled with the exaction of strict obedience to new norms prescribed by the liberal orthodoxy in another. In some matters, a charter of individual licence was granted which unleashed an unprecedented attack on old commonly held standards of personal behaviour and responsibility. . . .
>
> (Butt 1985)

The interesting point to note about a jeremiad such as this is not so much its strict accuracy – my own conviction is that it is in fact a distortion both of the decade and of the changes that have taken place – as its representative quality. The changes which the decade of the 1960s has come to stand for – a liberalization of attitudes, heightened individualism, greater freedom of sexual discussion, reforms of the law governing sexual behaviour, and so on – have become symbolic of wider transformation in our relation to traditional values. It matters little that the impact of the changes of the 1960s were limited at the time. They can be seen as harbingers of much wider transformations.

THE BREAKDOWN OF TRADITION

So what has changed? I suggest there are three broad areas where change has been rapid, and which have profoundly and irrevocably undermined traditional ways of being. The first I shall call the 'secularization' of sexuality. By this I mean the progressive detachment of sexual values from religious values – even for many of the religious. This has a long history, but possibly the key feature of its development was the process, beginning in the mid-nineteenth century, whereby the initiative for judging sexuality passed from the Churches to the agents of social and mental hygiene, primarily in the medical profession. This has been an unfinished revolution in the sense that moral and medical matters remain inextricably linked. You can still be singled out as sick and immoral if you offend our often unspoken norms. Nor, of course, do I intend to imply that the religious have given up their attempts to regulate sex. We only have to observe the rise of religious fundamentalism tied to moral authoritarianism in the _soi-disant_ Christian as well as the non-Christian worlds to counter that argument. Nevertheless, formal demarcations of what is right and proper, appropriate or inappropriate, have become increasingly the province of non-religious experts – in sexology, psychology, welfare services and social policy, as well as in medicine itself. Even in the most traditional of churches, such as the Roman Catholic, many of the faithful ignore their leaders' teaching on birth control, homosexuality or celibacy. Two of the most Catholic countries in Europe, Italy and Spain, have the lowest birth rates, suggesting that contraception in private life is the norm, whatever the public positions of priests. And, as we have seen, from America to Australia, Austria to Ireland, the Church hierarchy itself, under the most fiercely traditionalist of pontiffs, has been devastated by accusations of paedophilia in the priesthood. Similarly, the puritanical moral codes of the Islamic kingdom of Saudi Arabia have not stopped its princes haunting the pleasure pots of Western Europe. The fundamentalist emphasis on a rigid sexual code can be seen as, in part at least, a reaction to the dissolving impact of secularization. We reassert the value of that which is most threatened. But today we can reinvent the past and try to capture the future with the most advanced skills of the present. The new theocracies of the Islamic world may be fighting the whole thrust of modernity, but are doing so with the panoply of late modern technology which itself is contributing to the decline of the sacred. For the non-religious, attitudes have largely floated free of religious sanctions. The process of secularization has gone further in some countries (for example, Great Britain, despite having a national church) than in others (the USA, despite a formal separation of church and state). In all of them, however, the effect has been to place on sexual relations themselves a greater burden of expectation than hitherto. In the absence of any alternative world outlook to that of religion, sexuality itself has become an arena for thinking about personal destiny and belonging [2].

This tendency has been encouraged, and in part caused, by a related historical development. The new surge of expansive energy of world capitalism from the 1980s, which is linked to the wider process of globalization, has served to speed the dissolution of traditional structures, and to encourage the process of 'individualization' (Beck and Beck-Gernsheim 1995). There is a great historical irony in this. Some of the most prominent proponents of 'setting the individual free' to exploit the new market forces (Margaret Thatcher in Britain, Ronald Reagan in the USA) were moral conservatives and social authoritarians with regard to personal life. However, the very success of their economic ideologies served to fundamentally undermine their moral traditionalism. If you extol individual choice in economic matters, how can you resist the tide towards individual choice in matters concerning intimate life? Individualization is a social process which dis-embeds the individual from the weight but also from the protection of traditional structures. New opportunities but also new uncertainties are the inevitable result.

One significant effect of these major social developments is the drawing into commodity relations and relations of exchange of growing areas of 'private life'. The most spectacular example of this has been the vast growth of the market for pornography on a global scale since the 1950s. It is now a multi-billion-dollar industry, completely resilient to various efforts to eliminate it whether from traditionalists or feminists, and forcing ever more inventive means of regulation as the internet provides an amazingly efficient means of distribution. But there are other, more subtle areas of change. Patterns of courtship have been influenced by the commercialization of leisure. New technologies have shaped various aspects of personal life, from sex aids to reproductive technologies and designer drugs. Sex – especially female sexuality – has become a central feature of advertising, a vital element in the selling of everything from cigarettes to central heating. At the same time, new markets for sexual products have constantly been discovered or created – amongst adolescents in the 1950s, women in the 1960s, gays and lesbians in the 1980s and 1990s, and pre-pubescents in the present through the marketing of popular (for which read sexually inciting) music.

These changes have obviously increased the possibilities for exploitation, and their ill-effects can be seen in the form of degrading and objectifying imagery of women, in the seediness of the sex areas of major cities across the globe, in a romanticization of sexual violence, and the commercialization of sexual pleasures. Sex tourism has become one of the least appealing aspects of globalization, a new face to sexual colonialism and exploitation. Prostitution is a huge international industry, with sex workers often becoming commodities to be traded as part of the vast international flows of migration (e.g. Altman 2001; Seabrook 2001; O'Connell Davidson 1998). But for many millions of people escaping from social privation and sexual authoritarianism this new 'sexual freedom' has offered new possibilities. The changes of the past generations have acted like a solvent on old certainties and inherited values. They have opened the way to new dangers, providing ample scope for the rise of a new moralism. But they have also provided undreamt-of opportunities which many have seized.

Not surprisingly – and this is the second major trend – there has been a widespread *liberalization* of attitudes throughout the industrialized West and in the most modernized sections of the South of the globe, and an accompanying growth in toleration of individual difference, and acceptance of sexual diversity – especially among and by the young. People are generally more accepting of birth control, abortion, divorce, pre-marital sex, cohabitation of non-married partners and divorce, and of homosexuality. There has been a new recognition of the legitimacy of female sexuality. This does not mean there are not major areas of difficulty. The Roman Catholic hierarchy throughout the West has continued its opposition to non-marital sex, artificial birth control, abortion and divorce. Abortion has been a major divisive cause in the

USA. Sodomy laws still grace the statute books in certain American states, and in parts of Europe the law continues to treat homosexuality and heterosexuality differentially in age-of-consent laws and so on. Attitudes to teenage sexuality, and to enlightened sex education also vary enormously, with sometimes disastrous results. Countries like the USA, where sex education has become a significant political divide, and the UK, where attitudes to teenage sex remain ambivalent, tend to have much higher rates of teenage pregnancy than European countries like Holland, where sex education is efficient and taught early. Above all, perhaps, the changes of recent years have differentially affected men and women. There have indeed been greater opportunities for women to express their sexuality, a major encouragement of female sexual fulfilment. But in a culture in which the 'male in the head' continues to hold sway in many circumstances, this has often been in situations defined by men, for the benefit of men (Holland *et al.* 1998). Outside the highly developed countries, especially in those parts of the world which seek to define themselves against a corrupt or decadent west, the law of male dominance and of (often invented) tradition remains rampant. One thinks of the purges against homosexuality in Zimbabwe and parts of the Caribbean; the silencing of women in Taleban-dominated Afghanistan; the stoning to death of adulterers in Muslim-dominated parts of Nigeria; the many horrors of intolerance across the globe [3]. Genuine, radical tolerance, based on the full validation of different ways of being human, remains a precious gift of the few.

Nevertheless, in large parts of the world, on all standard measures of opinion, attitudes, if not universally non-authoritarian or non-exploitative, are certainly more varied and open than they were even a generation ago. This has been accompanied by an explosion of discourses around sexuality, a new willingness, and compulsion indeed, to speak about sex, to tell sexual stories in ever more inventive ways, resulting in an unprecedented profusion of sexual speech in everything from self-help literature and internet chat rooms to confessional television programmes. Homosexuality, the love that once dared not speak its name, has assumed an unprecedented volubility, and in its wake a profusion of sexual dissidents have spoken of their needs and rights in a new vocabulary of sexual desire. Nothing, it seems, is too esoteric or extreme to hide itself away from the insistent requirement to speak its truth – especially to the computer or the television camera. 'Sexuality' now speaks in many languages and modes, to and for many different types of people, offering a cacophony of alternative values and possibilities.

The effects of all this on *behaviour* are more difficult to gauge. There have, clearly, been significant changes in key life choices, particularly in the devaluation of marriage as the only legitimate gateway to adult sexual activity. In most Western countries certain common features have emerged. The vast majority of both men and women now have sexual relations before they are married. A very high proportion cohabit outside marriage, often in marriage-type relations (in countries like Sweden and Britain, the majority of children born to cohabiting couples are registered by both parents). A growing percentage have no intention of marrying; and increasing numbers of adults are living alone (approaching 25 per cent in Britain). But of course living alone does not imply an absence of sexual activity. People appear to be engaging in sexual activity on average earlier than their parents or grandparents. This is partly a result of earlier maturity in boys and girls (the age of menarche has come down from 16 to 13 in the past 100 years), partly a result of greater opportunity.

Yet surveys also demonstrate that despite significant shifts, individual behaviour remains fairly conservative. The high divorce figures (40 per cent of marriages in Britain) can be seen as a sign of the decline of marriage, but also as a desire to end failing relations in the hope of a better one. A high proportion of divorced people remarry – and remarry again if necessary. Serial monogamy not promiscuity is now the norm. Despite the higher profile of same-sex relations, the percentage of the population who see themselves as homosexual, or perhaps more accurately are willing to be open about their sexuality, appears (at 1 to 2 per cent) much smaller than many believed (or feared). And while the young may be having sex at an earlier age, their sexual practices remain hidebound by conservative beliefs about the right thing to do in male-female relations. Behaviour has lagged behind attitudes [4].

This has not prevented many commentators from seeing a 'crisis of the family' across the Western world, and beyond, partly as a result of changes in sexual mores. I would argue that there has indeed been a significant change in the *pattern of relationships*, and this constitutes the third major change. The perceived crisis has been traced to many roots and given various forms, but its focus has been an anxiety for the future of marriage, traditionally the privileged gateway to social status and sexual activity. After an increasing rate of marriage in the 1950s and early 1960s, a period when a higher percentage of men and women got married than ever before, a decline set in – in Sweden and Denmark from the mid-1960s, spreading to Britain, the USA and West Germany in the early 1970s, and France a little later. This was accompanied, as we have seen, by a rise in cohabitation and a steep increase in the incidence of divorce. Already by the early 1980s something like a third of marriages ended in divorce. In practice, fears of a collapse of marriage and the family proved somewhat premature. If 30 to 40 per cent of marriages promised to end in divorce up to two-thirds would still survive. Moreover, up to 70 per cent of the divorced remarry. Some sociologists saw signs in such figures not of the collapse of the traditional family, but of its re-emergence on new lines – the 'neo-conventional family' as it has sometimes been described: smaller than the Victorian family, with fewer children, possibly more equal in the distribution of domestic tasks, more prone perhaps to a pattern of 'serial monogamy' than in the past where marriage was, ideologically at least, for life. But it was still very recognizably 'a family'. Most people are still born into a family, most dwell most of their lives in one, and most people still aspire to found one. And in those parts of the world where kin ties are strong (as in southern Europe), family ties continue to be affirmed as fundamental.

All this is true, and very important for assessing our material and sexual culture. At the same time it is equally vital to recognize a growing diversity of domestic forms, cutting across the apparent solidity of the conventional family. Within the broad limits of the term 'family' itself there are many internal differences arising from different class, religious, racial, ethnic and political beliefs and practices. Alongside these different forms are various non-traditional patterns: never-married single-hood, non-marital cohabitation, voluntary childessness, 'the stepfamily' based on remarriage and the intermingling of children of different parents, single parenthood (within which term we must include both single-parent families created by divorce or death, and those created voluntarily, whether through conventional heterosexual intercourse, artificial insemination, or surrogacy), so-called 'open marriages', multi-adult households, gay and lesbian couples – and probably many more. It is wise today to refer not to the family, as if it were a fixed form, but to families, signifying diversity. In the absence of the agreed ground rules of tradition, people have no choice but to choose ways of life that are appropriate to them. The result for a growing number of people is 'life experiments' in which the simultaneous need for individual autonomy and mutual engagement with significant others create new patterns of living (Silva and Smart 1999; Weeks *et al.* 2001).

But even as diversity is a growing fact, we have not yet fully adapted to it either in ideology or social policy. Our culture is suffused by familial values, to the extent that the language of family still provides the only vocabulary of truly lasting relatedness that we have. It is surely significant that as lesbians and gays moved from a politics of identity in the 1970s to a politics of relationships and partnership rights in the 1990s and beyond, it was the language of 'families of choice' that emerged. The result of this is very curious and paradoxical. On the one hand there are many who bemoan the decline of 'the traditional family' and all that was associated with that. On the other, for the many who do not live in a conventional relationship, the ideology of the family still dominates to the extent that there is no real alternative legitimation to that of the family itself, no other way for expressing our need for relationships. The traditional connection between marriage, the family and sexuality has been in part severed; but in its place we have no obvious single alternative – rather a plurality of forms. For many this is a grave danger; for others it is the supreme challenge: to move from simply recognizing diversity as a fact to be endured, to seeing it as a value to be cherished.

LIVING WITH UNCERTAINTY: HIV/AIDS

The changes described above, while important, have not transformed the world of sexuality beyond recognition. Claims either of 'sexual liberation' or of 'moral decline' would seem to be wide of the mark. Yet the very subtlety and ambivalence of change has contributed to a crisis of values and of meanings, a climate of uncertainty and (for some) confusion. In such a climate deep currents of feeling come to the surface and find expression in what are called moral panics. Moral panics are flurries of social anxiety, usually focusing on a condition or person, or group of persons, who become defined as a threat to accepted social values and assumptions. They arise generally in situations of confusion and ambiguity, in periods when the boundaries between legitimate and illegitimate behaviour seem to need redefining or classification. Classic moral panics in the past have often produced drastic results, in the form of moral witch-hunts, physical assault and legislative action. Since the Second World War there has been an apparently endless series, many of them focusing on moral and sexual issues: over venereal disease, prostitution, homosexuality, child sex abuse and paedophilia, teenage sex, pornography, and so on. A significant feature in many of them has been the connection that has been made between sex and disease, disease becoming a metaphor for dirt, disorder and decay. Not surprisingly, panics have emerged over the social and moral connotations of genital herpes, cervical cancer and most recently and dramatically of all, HIV and AIDS. Particularly in the early 1980s, when the first signs of an unprecedented epidemic emerged amongst the male gay population of the USA, the reaction to AIDS illustrated all the characteristic signs of a classic panic. More important for our discussion here, it revealed also the wider anxieties abroad about the current place of sexuality in our society. The resulting crisis threw light on many dark corners of our sexual culture, condensing a number of social stresses into a recognizable symbolic target [5]. As the epidemic raged worldwide in the decades that followed, taking millions of people to a premature grave, and even threatening a fundamental breakdown in economic life in some parts of the world, the dangerous connection of sexuality, disease and death has put the erotic to an unprecedented trial.

One of the most striking features of the HIV/AIDS crisis was that, unlike most illnesses, from the first the people who were affected by it, and had to live and die with it, were chiefly blamed for causing the syndrome, whether because of their social attitudes or sexual practices. And as most people suffering from HIV/AIDS at the beginning of the epidemic in Western countries were male homosexuals, this was highly revealing about current attitudes and feelings towards unorthodox sexualities. From the earliest identification of the disease in America in 1981–82, AIDS was addressed as if it were a peculiarly homosexual affliction, and the term 'gay plague' became the common description of it in the more scabrous parts of the media. In fact it was clear from the beginning that other groups of people were prone to the disease: Haitians (in the USA) and intravenous drug abusers, and haemophiliacs, because of their dependence on other people's blood. It soon became apparent, too, that in large parts of central Africa, where the disease may have originated, and where it seemed to be endemic, it was the heterosexual

population that was chiefly afflicted and it was therefore clearly trans-
mittable through heterosexual intercourse. But it was the apparent
connection between unorthodox sexual activity and the disease that
chiefly fuelled the major elements of panic in the industrialized West,
and for long coloured responses across the globe.

In the normal course of a moral panic there is a characteristic
stereotyping of the main actors as peculiar types of monsters, leading
to an escalating level of fear and perceived threat, the taking up of
panic stations and absolutist positions, and a search for symbolic, and
usually imaginary solutions to the dramatized problem. In the case
of AIDS there was a genuinely appalling disease, which devastated the
lives of many people, for which there was no cure, and which at first
seemed unstoppable in its rate of spread. By mid-1985 it had become
the largest single cause of adult male deaths in New York City and
was widespread elsewhere. Anxiety was legitimate. However, the form
that the anxiety took was a search for scapegoats, and here gay men
were peculiarly vulnerable. Certain sexual practices (for example anal
intercourse) and social habits (multiple partners) generally (though
often misleadingly) associated with male homosexuals were given a
prime role in the spread of the disease, and it became easy to attribute
blame to people with AIDS. From this a slippage readily took place:
between the idea that homosexuals *caused* 'the plague' (itself without
any backing in evidence) to the idea that homosexuality itself was a
plague. Manifestations of what Susan Sontag has called 'practices of
decontamination' against the vulnerable soon appeared (Sontag 1983,
1989): restaurants refused to serve gay customers, gay waiters were
sacked, dentists refused to examine the teeth of homosexuals, rubbish
collectors wore masks when collecting garbage from suspected victims,
prison officers refused to move prisoners, backstage staff in theatres
refused to work with gay actors, distinguished pathologists refused to
examine the bodies of AIDS patients, and undertakers refused to bury
them.

The scientific evidence already by the mid-1980s was clear: AIDS was
carried by a virus, which was not in itself exceptionally infectious. It was
only possible to catch it through intimate sexual contact or interchange
of blood. It was not a peculiarly homosexual disease, and most people
in the world with the disease were in fact heterosexual. Moreover, its
spread could, in all likelihood, be hindered by relatively small changes

in lifestyle, particularly the avoidance of certain sexual practices (such as anal intercourse without protection). All this suggested that what was needed was a public education campaign which both allayed fears and promoted an awareness of safer sexual activities. Eventually, across the rich and highly developed world, this is what happened (Altman 1994; Haour-Knipe and Rector 1996; Moatti *et al.* 2000). But not before fear and ignorance produced a fervour of punitive responses. And as the pandemic spread inexorably across the globe, the pattern of fear, blame, wilful neglect, inconsistent response followed – with a vital difference: whereas in the richer parts of the world, safer sex practices stemmed the spread of HIV and expensive cocktails of drugs proved effective in slowing down the impact of multiple illnesses, in the majority of the world the epidemic was inextricably linked with poverty and a web of other diseases. As in the West the reaction to the HIV/AIDS epidemic shone a revealing light on deep-rooted anxieties and a prevailing climate of uncertainty, so in the rest of the world, the epidemic revealed structural inequalities, exploitation, and the hazards of unprecedented sexual change. Vast disruptions of population in response to rapid industrialization, moves from country to city, migrations across borders, flight in the wake of war, eased the spread of sexual and blood-borne infections. Ignorance (for example, the apparent widespread belief in southern Africa that sex with a virgin would cure sexual infections) or prejudice (against condoms on the grounds that they were unmanly) helped rapid spread. Transnational travel carried the epidemic from continent to continent. By 2002 there were 42 million people in the world living with HIV and AIDS, of whom over half were women. UNAIDS, the international body coordinating the fight against the epidemic, described the spread of HIV in southern Africa as 'rampant'. At the beginning of 2003 there were two million HIV/AIDS orphans living in southern Africa, and eleven million more in sub-Saharan Africa. From South America to Southeast Asia, from Eastern Europe to China and India, new epidemics threatened, threatening economic and social collapse, population decline, and ever greater numbers of orphaned children [6].

In the face of so much horror it is difficult to find resources for hope. And yet they can be found. Starting in the gay communities of Western cities, but spreading throughout the globe, there was an unprecedented mobilization of community-based responses to HIV and AIDS, ranging from self-instruction in safer sex to advocacy and campaigning. Those most affected often took the lead in combating the epidemic. In the face of disease and death, many people found means of living their lives well. The international mobilization against HIV and AIDS, whether through official bodies like UNAIDS or in proliferating NGOs, helped to develop an international discourse around sexual risk and sexual health – though frequently against the backdrop of state ignorance and neglect. Haphazardly and hesitantly at first, Western expertise and drugs began to alleviate some of the worst suffering. And sexual practices and identities that had been hidden in shame began to find their voice, and open themselves to history, and therefore change. HIV/AIDS, an unprecedented crisis in sexual behaviour, had an uncanny way of revealing the contradictions, confusions, ambiguities, cruelties and opportunities in our relationship to the sexual. It is perhaps not surprising that the initial reaction was fear and panic. All one can say is that combating HIV/AIDS requires much more than that: above all, an understanding of the significance of sexuality in contemporary cultures, and an ability to face its challenges openly and honestly (see Altman 1994; Weeks 1995).

REGULATING SEXUALITY

The crisis of sexual meanings has accentuated the problem of how to regulate and control sexuality. What we believe sexuality is, or ought to be, structures our responses to it. So it is difficult to separate the particular meanings we give to sex from the forms of control we advocate. If we regard sex as dangerous, disruptive and fundamentally antisocial, then we are likely to embrace moral and political positions which propose tight, authoritarian regulation. This I shall call the absolutist position. If, on the other hand, we believe that the powers of desire are basically benign, life-enhancing and liberating we are liable to adopt a relaxed, even radical set of values, to support a libertarian stance. Somewhere between these two extreme positions we will find a third: it is perhaps rather less certain about whether sex in itself is good or bad; it is convinced, however, of the evils both of moral authoritarianism and of excess. This I shall call the liberal or liberal-pluralist position. These three approaches – or strategies of regulation – have all been present in our culture for a long time. They still largely provide the framework – whether consciously or subliminally – for current debates about sex and politics.

discuss

Historically, we are heirs of the absolutist tradition. This has been based on a fundamental belief that the disruptive powers of sex can only be controlled by a clear-cut morality, intricately embedded in a particular set of social institutions: marriage, heterosexuality, family life and (at least in the Judaic-Christian traditions) monogamy. This absolutist morality is deeply rooted in the Christian West and in the Islamic East, but though its grounding may be in faith, it is today a much wider cultural and political phenomenon, embraced as readily by the atheist as by the Christian (or other religious) who is ready to worship at the foot of strong, moral values. Moral absolutism has deeply influenced our general culture, and in particular the forms of legal regulation, many of which still survive. The major set of legal changes in countries like Britain in the last decades of the nineteenth century and the early part of the twentieth century (on obscenity, prostitution, age of consent, homosexuality, incest) were pushed for by absolutist social morality movements, propelled in many cases by a religious fervour, and frequently in alliance with moral feminism. Though tempered by selective enforcement and pragmatic adjustments (for example on prostitution, where moralistic censure and tacit acceptance lived side by side), these laws continued to define sexual offences until the 1960s, and sometimes beyond. A similar pattern can be seen in the USA and other English-speaking countries, and, other things being equal, in many European countries as well (Weeks 1989). As we have seen, there has been a significant revival of absolutist positions allied both to the rise of a New Right in the USA from the 1970s and 1980s, and to the wave of fundamentalism across the globe. This has produced surprising alliances in international sexual politics. The Roman Catholic Church had no difficulty in allying with Islamic countries in attempting to block an advancing agenda on reproductive rights at the International Conference on Population and Development in the early 1990s (Neale 1998). Access to birth control and abortion by women, linked to a gender revolution and to dramatic changes in familial relations, undermined absolutist, traditional values, and had to be resisted.

Like the absolutist approach, the libertarian tradition embraces various strands of belief. It can be found as much on the political right as on the political left. One important element has a surprising affinity, in its fundamental assumptions about what sex is, to moral absolutism. A major literary tradition, from the Marquis de Sade through the 'decadents' of the late nineteenth century to more or less contemporary writers such as Georges Bataille and Jean Genet, celebrates sex as danger and transgression. Like the Christian absolutists they appear to see sexuality as threatening the self, the society and even the universe. Unlike the absolutists they believe it should [7]. Transgressive sex is a way of breaking out of the tyranny of the existing order, of smashing the artificial boundaries between people and bodies, between sexualities, imposed by the sexual tradition. Here they join hands (despite often pronounced theoretical differences) with another libertarian strand, who similarly believe that sexual liberation is a (perhaps *the*) key to social freedom, a disruptive energy that can help break the existing order. The difference is that these libertarians believe that sex is fundamentally good and healthy, a force blocked only by the power of 'civilization' or capitalism. There is often here a close affinity with a strong socialist tradition, stretching from pioneers like Charles Fourier and Edward Carpenter to Wilhelm Reich in the 1930s and Herbert Marcuse in the 1950s and 1960s. Such a political libertarianism had enormous influence in the developing sexual politics of the late 1960s. It is on the opposite side of the political spectrum from a third strand of libertarianism, which has grown in significance since the 1970s, a right wing libertarianism linked to an almost absolutist individualism. If, as many right wing theorists argue, the state and its colonizing agenda is the real enemy of individual freedom, then the less the weight of prohibitions and restrictions on individual action the better. Hence an agenda which is willing to deregulate all forms of drug use as well as hitherto tabooed sexual behaviour, including in some cases paedophilia [8].

The problem with the absolutist and libertarian traditions is that they all take for granted fundamentally essentialist views about what sex is. Sexuality in itself appears not only as a powerful energy which is outside and opposed to society, but also, because of this, a natural force which appears to embody its own morality. Values and theoretical assumptions about the nature of sex are closely related. In this sense, libertarianism and absolutism are mirror-images of one another: both are committed to a view of sexuality which transcends the bounds of mere history.

In practice, however, the regulation of sexuality in most late modern societies for the past generation has been dominated by varying forms of the liberal tradition. I say 'varying forms' because there are considerable shifts of interpretation between one culture and another, with different emphases particularly apparent between North America and Europe. In the United States the central organizing idea has been that of 'rights': it is significant, for example, that in the debates over abortion each side uses the language of fundamental rights, the rights of the unborn child versus the rights of the mother to control over her body. As this illustrates, to speak of rights does not end the discussion. We are still left with the problem of which person's rights are paramount in what specific situation, and whose rights are taken up can often be a clearly political rather than an *a priori* moral issue. In the case of abortion there are conflicting values at play. The result is a battle between rival absolutes in which each side has only its own passion and ability to mobilize support to rely on.

In Britain, on the other hand, the idea of fundamental civil rights was not enshrined either in a written constitution, or until the turn of the Millennium in any statute enshrining fundamental human rights. It was partly through the involvement of the UK in the European Union that a rights discourse began to circulate and influence sexual policy (e.g. Bell 1998). The liberal tradition therefore developed pragmatically, and took a different path from that of the USA. It is, nevertheless, very deeply entrenched, and in relationship to sexuality is has been very clearly and influentially articulated – most famously in the Wolfenden Committee report on prostitution and male homosexuality, published in 1957 (Home Office 1957). The point of confluence with the American tradition is in the emphasis both approaches put on achieving an appropriate balance between private and public spheres. The Wolfenden report made the distinction classically clear. It was, it proposed, the duty of the law to regulate the public sphere, and in particular to maintain public decency. There were limits, however, in its obligation to control the private sphere, the traditional arena of personal morality. Churches might strive to tell people what to do in their private lives. It was not the task of the state to attempt to do the same. The state, therefore, had no place in the enforcement of private standards. In such an approach there was a tacit acceptance that society was no longer – if it ever had been – governed by a moral consensus, and that there was in practice a plurality of alternative moral views abroad. The law should therefore limit its role to the maintenance of common standards of public decency.

The 'Wolfenden strategy' provided the theoretical framework for the series of reforms concerning sexuality that were enacted in Britain in the 1960s: reforms in the laws on obscenity, homosexuality, abortion, theatre censorship and divorce (see Weeks 1989: ch. 13). Their starting point was the belief that absolutist approaches were inadequate for regulating sexuality, because there was no common morality to underpin them. It was striking that most of the leading Christian Churches, especially those closely related to the established order like the Church of England, endorsed this assumption: they may not have approved of homosexuality, abortion or divorce, but they clearly believed that they could no longer expect the law itself to enshrine this moral position.

There was more than a simple moral agnosticism in this rationalized approach. There was also an implicit feeling that the law itself was no longer, if it had ever been, an appropriate or effective means for attempting to control private sexual behaviour. There was a search in many of the debates around sexuality in the period for alternative methods of regulation, which concentrated on limiting harm rather than eliminating sin. Havelock Ellis had already articulated the characteristic approach in the 1930s: 'The question is no longer: Is the act abnormal? It becomes: Is the act injurious?' (Ellis 1946: 183). The Wolfenden report itself discussed whether homosexuality and prostitution could be regarded as sicknesses, best treated by medicine rather than law. It concluded that they were not diseases, but nevertheless advocated further research into their 'aetiologies' (origins and development), and one of the assumptions of the reformers who followed was that medicine or welfare agencies were better placed than the legal authorities to properly regulate sexuality: it was doctors in the abortion reform law of 1967 who were given the prime responsibility for deciding whether a woman should or should not be allowed termination of her pregnancy, not the woman herself.

The reforms conformed, then, to a liberal strategy which limited direct interference in private lives. But they did not necessarily abandon the idea of control – the law was actually tightened in relationship to public displays of prostitution and homosexuality – nor did they positively enshrine new rights. There was no abortion on demand, no legally enshrined right to divorce by mutual consent, and male homosexuality was not fully legalized: certain types of homosexual behaviour, between consenting adults (over 21) in private, were decriminalized but not legitimized, and this was representative. It was to take until 2001 for the age of consent for heterosexuals and non-heterosexuals to be equalized at 16. Just as the liberal approach was agnostic on the effectiveness of the law in a complex society, so it was agnostic about the merits of the activities it directed its attention towards.

The reforms of the 1960s were of great importance and they certainly provided the preconditions for many of the changes in the generation that followed. Some of the results were spectacular. Between 1968 and 1980 over a million legal abortions were carried out in Britain. The divorce rate trebled for those under 25 between 1970 and 1979, and doubled for those over 25. New possibilities opened up for discussing sex, in books and the theatre, and for developing new lifestyles. But changes did not all go in one direction. At the same time as male homosexuality was decriminalized, which for the first time made possible a publicly affirmed homosexual way of life, between 1967 and 1976 the recorded incidents of indecency between men doubled, the number of prosecutions trebled and the number of convictions quadrupled. Several attempts were made to limit abortions. The divorce legislation led to agitated efforts to come to terms with the child-care and financial consequences. This illustrates what Stuart Hall has called 'the double taxonomy' of freedom *and* control that lay behind the reforms (Hall 1980).

Nevertheless, the reforms themselves became symbolic of all the other changes that were taking place, and the sticking point for those who wanted to halt the tide of liberalism and permissiveness. In the USA where, true to tradition, reforms had been achieved through court action rather than law changes, the key decision of the Supreme Court in 1973 to allow abortion became the occasion for what has been described as a 'moral civil war' between contending forces. The resulting 'culture wars' became a fundamental divide about what America was and should be (e.g. Herman 1997; Duggan and Hunter 1995). In Britain the 1960s reforms became the target for vigorous attempts at restrictive amendment, and, even more critically, set targets for conservative counter-attacks.

One of the difficulties of the liberal strategy in out-facing these challenges was that, while it certainly disturbed conservative moralists, the approach did not on the whole engage the energetic support of radical forces, largely because of its hesitant or narrow endorsement of sexual pluralism. Moreover, the approach itself had severe weaknesses when faced with the growing complexities of sex-related questions in the face of rapid change. The difficulties of the Wolfenden strategy were strikingly illustrated by the reaction to the new reproductive technologies in the early 1980s: the problems posed, in particular, by artificial insemination by donor (AID), by in vitro fertilization (IVF) and the use of surrogate mothers, and by embryological research. The report of the Warnock Committee on human fertilization and embryology, in grappling with these issues, observed that there were two levels to the debate (Warnock 1985). The first was the issue of whether there could be general agreement that an action was right or wrong in itself (for example, surrogacy or AID). The second was the still more difficult problem that, even if there was unanimity over a particular activity, would it be justified to intervene to enforce a moral view? On the question, say, of research using human embryos, the classic liberal distinctions between private pleasure and public policy could not operate. The desire for positive results from embryological research might be a private goal (encouraged by the hope, for example, of finding a clue to certain genetically transmitted illnesses) but it was likely to be publicly financed, and therefore the subject of political decisions. At the same time it raised appallingly difficult ethical questions about the nature of life and the obligations of science.

In a case such as this the provision of a formal framework for separating the law and private morality could not in itself be a satisfactory method for dealing with difficult questions of choice or conflicts of values. Not surprisingly, questions of how embryological research should be controlled, and about the merits of commercial surrogacy, became immediate political controversies cutting across conventional party divisions and transcending traditional liberal alliances. These controversies were the harbingers of even more difficult dilemmas as technology became ever more sophisticated in intervening in the processes of reproduction, and as the genetic revolution opened up the at least theoretical possibility of eliminating embryos that might carry 'harmful' genes. If such a thing as a gay gene existed, should parents have the right to abort the unborn child that might carry it? Should parents have the right to choose the gender of their offspring? Should surrogacy be open to gay male parents as well as heterosexual ones? Such questions illustrate again that politics, morality and sexuality do not inhabit separate spheres of social life. They are intimately and inextricably connected in the actual political and social climate in which we live.

TOWARDS SEXUAL CITIZENSHIP

The usefulness of seeing sexuality as shaped in culture is that it allows us to recognize the contingency and arbitrariness of our own social arrangements. It does not, however, tell us how we should live today. Given these uncertainties, it is not surprising that a great deal of contemporary debate focuses on intimate relationships. The so-called crisis of the family is not simply about changes in domestic patterns. It is about the relationships between men and women, men and men, women and women, adults and children. This leads to fundamental questions. Has there, as theorists like Giddens and Beck and Beck-Gernsheim suggest, been a basic shift in the relationship of men and women towards new patterns of egalitarian intimacy? To what extent does the emergence of non-heterosexual families of choice represent an augury of more egalitarian and chosen lifestyles? To what extent are the sharp dichotomies between heterosexuality and homosexuality dissolving in a post-familial world (Giddens 1992; Beck and Beck-Gernsheim 1995)? These questions have become the subject of controversy as we try to make sense of values and behaviours that are changing before our eyes.

What is clear is that debates about sexualities must in the end be debates about relationships, about intimacy, and about the values of everyday life. Despite the best fantasies of prophets of the internet and of cybersex (Wolmark 1999), sexuality is always ultimately about interaction with others. It is through that interaction that the meanings of sexuality are shaped, and what we know as sexuality is produced. It is surely interesting therefore that the stories we tell each other about sexuality and intimate life are themselves changing.

There has been a proliferation of sexual stories since the eighteenth century, but only in the late twentieth century have these stories gained a mass audience. The sexual stories we tell are deeply implicated in moral and political change, and shifting stories of self, identity and relationships carry the potential, as Plummer has argued, for radical transformations of the social order (Plummer 1995). They are circulated in and through social movements and communities, and become the focus for thinking through and reorientating the needs and desires of everyday life. Over the past generation we have seen a change in the forms and organization of the stories we tell each other, and late modern stories reveal and create a multiplicity of new projects, new constituencies, new possibilities for the future. These are stories of human life chances, of emotional and sexual democracy, of pluralistic forms of sexual life, opening the way for a new culture of intimacy and what increasingly is described as sexual or 'intimate' citizenship (Evans 1985; Weeks 1998; Plummer 2002).

Sexual/intimate citizenship, like all forms of citizenship, is about belonging, about rights and responsibilities, about ending social exclusion and ensuring social inclusion. It is concerned with equity and justice. Traditionally, claims to citizenship have been based on ensuring civil, political, social and economic rights. Under the impact of feminism a global discourse on women's rights has profoundly shifted the global debate on citizenship, putting gender right at the heart of debates. In a global sense the traditional battles for full equality in civil, political, social and economic rights have yet to be fully won, but there is now a widespread recognition that these cannot be separated from issues of sexuality. The international movement for reproductive rights puts sexuality and sexual rights at the centre of a nexus of intersecting lines of power, demonstrating the variety of local, national and global forces, and conflicting aspirations, which shape women's claims to self-determination in relation to their bodies. In the same way, the lesbian and gay movement has become global in scope, taking on different local colour, adapting to different configurations of oppression/suppression/opportunity. In both cases, the claim to full citizenship necessarily embraces new claims for rights [9]. And in many parts of the world, these rights are being recognized.

Local gains are often countered by national losses, especially when conservative political forces resume power. Similarly, national gains can be thwarted by local resistances, and battles over space. A major part of sexual politics is played out in daily struggles over what can be said or performed by whom in what circumstances in a multitude of battle grounds, where differences of power are ritualistically acted out with the aim of excluding the transgressor (Bell and Valentine 1995). As befits a long revolution, two steps forward are followed by one step backwards. Uneven development takes its toll. Yet it seems to me undeniable that the past couple of generations have seen an unprecedented and almost certainly irreversible shift in values and practices, which in turn is being reflected in the achievement of citizenship rights. There is plentiful evidence, for example, which suggests a widespread acceptance of the merits of companionate and more equal relationships, even as we fail to achieve them fully in our everyday life. As Giddens argued, the egalitarian relationship has become a measure by which increasing numbers of people feel they must judge their own individual lives (Giddens 1992). At the centre of this ideal is the fundamental belief that love relationships and partnerships should be a matter not of arrangement or tradition, but of personal choice based on a balance of attraction, desire, mutual trust and compatibility.

These new stories of intimacy that are now increasingly shaping our culture can be seen in part, as I suggested above, as examples of a new or accentuated individualism in most Western societies. The economic and cultural changes in the past generation have tended to exalt the individual over the collective, elevating individual self-expression and material well-being, and undermining many of the traditional sources of solidarity. This individualism, as we have seen, has had its effect on family and sexual life. The triumph of economic liberalism has tended to undermine traditional patterns. This new individualism has aroused extreme anxieties amongst moral conservatives. It has left more generally an underlying sense of unease, which is manifest in recurrent 'moral panics' around sexual issues. Yet whatever the undercurrent of uncertainty, most people, perforce, have to negotiate the rapids of change, and without recourse to transcendent value system, or tradition.

Most people in the West are not particularly interested in politics or the politics of family and sexuality in particular. They do not have grand visions of new ways of living, even as at an everyday level they do engage in 'experiments in living'. There is pragmatism in the adaptation to changes in everyday life, and a new contingency as people have, in a real sense, to create values for themselves. People's liberalism may well be limited to a form of live and let live morality. There is no positive endorsement of different ways of life. Yet there are very few households across the richer parts of the world which are not touched by the transformations of everyday life. Most people know single parents. Most people know a member of their family who may be lesbian or gay. Most households have experienced divorce, remarriage, cohabitation, broken families, reconstituted families. We are in the midst, as I have argued, of a genuine social revolution. The revolution is unfinished, partial, uneven in its impact. But we all now have to live with the consequences and implications. And the evidence surely is that most people adapt surprisingly well.

The lesson of the past generation is that the dramatic changes with regard to family and sexual life have not been led by the political elite but by grassroots shifts which are subject to a whole variety of long-term social trends. Governments, of course, have to respond, but they inevitably do so in a variety of different ways, depending on political traditions, the prevailing balance of cultural forces, the nature of the political institutions, the day-to-day crises which force some issues to the fore, and the pressure from below, whether from conservative or fundamentalist resistance to change, or from radical social movements.

I have argued elsewhere that such movements, like the lesbian and gay movements, which are rooted in everyday life, characteristically veer between 'moments of transgression' and 'moments of citizenship' (Weeks 1995: 108–23). The first highlights the factors that make for social exclusion, and the drama of difference. The second makes the claim for social inclusion, for recognition, for full belonging. In practice, the two moments constantly flow into each other, reinforcing one another. Neither one can work without the other. The debate over same-sex partnerships, marriage and chosen families, illustrates some of the tensions and ambiguities that claims to sexual or intimate citizenship inevitably involve. Is same-sex marriage necessary because it will mark the full integration of lesbians and gays into society, as gay conservatives argue? Or desirable because it mimics, undermines and transgresses the heterosexual institution, as queer activists might argue? Should gay families be acknowledged because we all need families, or because they subvert the concept of the traditional family as the foundation stone of society (Weston 1991; Weeks *et al.* 2001; Wintermute and Andenaes 2001)?

The reality is that across the world many thousands are making choices about how they want to live on a day-by-day basis. Most of them are not particularly preoccupied by theoretical or theological disputes. They are concerned, however, that they can live their chosen lives with openness and legitimacy, that indeed they have the full freedom to choose, so that they can make their life decisions with a sense of mutual care, responsibility, respect, and transparency. Through their voices, in their stories, and the stories of thousands in similar positions, we see new claims being articulated, circulated and re-circulated, creating new communities of knowledge and empowerment, new realities. Through the vicissitudes of everyday, intimate life, new ways of living, life experiments, are being constructed. And slowly, often painfully, with due hesitation, sexual rights are being written into law. We are learning, at last, to live with sexual diversity, and are beginning to realize the meaning of full sexual citizenship.

a bit optimistic, whiggish & self-congratulatory!

6

PRIVATE PLEASURES AND PUBLIC POLICY

> If human nature is historical, individuals have different histories and
> therefore different needs.
>
> Michael Ignatieff (1984: 135)

There are many questions we could ask about sexuality: about duty and
choice, morality and immorality, goodness and evil, health and sickness,
truth and falsity. Subtle, and not so subtle, debates around some or all of
these dichotomies have dominated the Western discourse on sexuality
for over two thousand years. Whatever the range of answers that may
be reached, they all have the distinction of carrying a heavy weight of
prescription, of telling people, often very coercively, how they must
behave in order to attain the good (or moral or hygienic) life. The
unifying thread of this essay, however, is that the idea of sexuality has
been loaded down with too many assumptions, that it has lumbered
under a weight of expectations it cannot, and should not have to, bear.
'Sex acts', Gayle Rubin has rightly said, 'are burdened with an excess of
significance' (Rubin 1984: 285). We should lighten the load.

One of the major difficulties in doing this has been the privileged role
claimed by the experts on sex over the past hundred years in telling us

what is good or bad, appropriate or inappropriate behaviour. In his Presidential address to the 1929 Congress of the World League for Sexual Reform, Magnus Hirschfeld declared that: 'A sexual ethics based on science is the only sound system of ethics' (Hirshchfeld 1930: xiv). The impulse behind this statement was noble indeed. Hirschfeld, like other luminaries of this first phase of the sexological revolution, looked forward to a new enlightenment in which prejudice, religious moralism, and authoritarian sexual codes would dissolve before the light of reason as provided by the new science of sex. Sexual knowledge and sexual politics marched hand in hand as the sexologists, like Hirschfeld, Havelock Ellis and Auguste Forel (joint Presidents of the World League in 1929) also became the patrons of sex reform, while sexual reformers of various hues, from feminist birth controllers to campaigners for homosexual rights, looked to the scientists for guidelines to further their activities. 'Through science to Justice', Hirschfeld famously proclaimed as the watchword of his Scientific-Humanitarian Committee. It was the motto of the whole sex reform movement. The problem then, as now, was that the insights of this new science were not straightforward or unequivocal: to put it bluntly, sexologists disagreed with one another. Homosexual activists might look to Hirschfeld's theories which said that they belonged to a biologically given 'third' or 'intermediate' sex to justify their claims to social justice, but the Nazis who burned Hirschfeld's library and legacy after 1933 could equally well use more or less the same arguments to disqualify homosexuals altogether, as biological anomalies, from the new moral order – and find scientists only too willing to support them. Sexologists might point out the fact that sexuality was a rich and varied continent, but they also lent their weight to normalizing institutions, to attempts at 'cures', and to eugenic solutions to the 'problems' of overpopulation and the proliferation of the 'feeble-minded'. Havelock Ellis was not alone in being a sexual reformer, and also a supporter of the eugenic breeding of 'the best' (inevitably defined by class and racial criteria). The proliferating literature on married love might encourage the belief that women, too, were sexual beings deserving of satisfaction and pleasure. But these marriage experts also managed to pathologize the single woman and to sustain a burgeoning literature on the inadequacies of 'frigid' women.

The ultimate political and moral implications of sexual enlightenment were at best ambiguous and at worst dangerous as they contributed a scientific justification for essentially traditional or authoritarian positions. By the 1920s social purity organizations were looking to the writings of Ellis, Freud and others to underpin their modified but still fundamentally normalizing positions. Over the decades since, the science of sex has been drawn upon to justify a huge variety of moral positions, from passionate advocacy of sexual revolution to fervent endorsement of sexual orthodoxy. Today, even the least theoretical of moral entrepreneurs is able to call on an encyclopaedia of would-be-scientific arguments to sustain her or his position, from hormonal theories, evolutionary psychology and the 'silent whisperings' of sociology for explaining sexual difference and perversity and to justify the inevitability of inequality. It is particularly interesting in this regard that when the case was being made for the existence of the gay gene by gay activists, who thought it could be used to justify their own existence, the enemies of diversity sought to use the same evidence to welcome the possibility of eliminating the gene by genetic engineering.

This is not a polemic aimed at the rejection of any attempt at a scientific understanding of the workings of the body or the mind. It is, however, an argument for abandoning the claim that a self-styled science of sex alone provides an objective guide into the truth of our bodies, and hence a code by which we should live our personal and social lives. The 'science of sex', like every other science, is enmeshed in the web of social relations. We should accordingly treat its more extravagant claims, especially when it is dealing with humans in all their contrariness, with caution and a sensitivity to their origins. As Steven Epstein has demonstrated in relation to the science of HIV/AIDS, the subjects of scientific investigation have their own voices, and are not prepared to simply accept what they are told as the final truth. We are in the midst of a struggle over who can speak legitimately about the body, its needs and desires (Epstein 1996).

Against the sexual tradition which sexology has done so much to sustain I have sought in this essay to *problematize* the idea of sexuality, to show its emergence from an intricate history, its close implication in relations of power, its deployment to sustain and normalize certain forms of erotic activity and its marginalization of others, and the crisis of meanings that has resulted from the diverse challenges which it has generated. But we are still left with a question which looms ever larger as we contemplate the domain of sexuality: what should the place of sex be in our individual lives in the contemporary world? This is scarcely a minor question. At its heart is the old, old question of ethics, of how we should live.

The critique of reductionist views of sexuality which underpins this work has been very useful in casting light on hidden but controlling assumptions, and in opening up the sexual field to new questions, about history, power, meanings, diversity, choice and so on. It has, on the whole, been less successful in providing maps for navigating the highways and byways of what is still, despite all the torrents of writing about it, a partly uncharted country. The reason for this lack is quite straight-forward. Sexology offered an alternative world outlook to the religious cosmology much of its initial energy was directed against. It claimed to be uncovering the truth of Nature in opposition to the truths of mere prejudice or tradition. But if scientific knowledge itself is suspect, what is left?

If we reject the hierarchy of sexual values laid down by the science of sex, how do we distinguish between the normal and the abnormal? If, as Foucault said with reference to Sade, 'sex is without any norm or intrinsic rule that might be formulated from its own nature' (Foucault 1979: 149), how do we determine appropriate and inappropriate behaviour? If we can no longer regard sex as either intrinsically threatening and evil, or liberating and good, how can we escape the Scylla of moralism on the one hand and the Charybdis of anything-goes libertarianism on the other? Finally, if we can no longer accept the politics of the old 'sexual revolutionaries' because of their reductive view of sexuality, and not believe in a transcendent 'sexual liberation', because of the inevitable involvement of sex in the intricate play of power, what are sexual politics for? Recent liberation movements, Foucault observed in a late interview, 'suffer from the fact that they cannot find any principle on which to base the elaboration of the new ethics . . . [other than] an ethics founded on so-called scientific knowledge of what the self is, what desire is, what the unconscious is, and so on' (Foucault 1984: 343). The trouble is that this 'scientific knowledge' is, as we know, full of divisions and contradictions about what the self is, what desire may be, and even whether there is such a thing as 'the unconscious'. Yet if we reject these guidelines, is there anything left?

Foucault's own late attempt to grapple with this dilemma, in the two volumes of his *History* published at the very end of his life, is characteristically indirect. The two volumes are superficially at least simple exegeses of ancient Greek and Latin texts on how people should live (Foucault 1985, 1986). But their very indirection and lack of obvious contact with today's problems serves to clarify what is at stake. He likens the world of the Greeks and Romans to our own in one key respect. Like us post-Christians, they were faced with the task of elaborating an ethic that was not founded in religion or any other *a priori* justification, least of all science. Like us they were troubled with moral questions around what we term sexuality (the nearest equivalent for them was called *aphrodisia*). Many of the concerns have in fact been continuous for over 2,000 years: with the body, the relations of men and women, of men and men. Unlike us, however, they did not attempt a codification of acts which made sex itself the bearer of negative values and moral anxieties, nor attempt a subordination of individuals to external rules of conduct based on such values and anxieties. They sought instead an 'aesthetics of existence', an art of life in which temperance balanced excess, self-discipline kept pleasures in order.

The ancients were preoccupied with methods of self-knowledge, with techniques of the self, rules of conduct organized around dietary matters (the individual's relation with his body), economics (the conduct of the head of the household) and the erotic (the relations of men and boys). They were, in other words, seeking modes of life which derived not from a central truth about sex, but from the set of relations in which the individual was embedded. The aim was to define the uses of pleasure in a way which neither ignored it, nor surrendered to its intoxicating force.

Foucault is not of course suggesting that this is a model for our own time. This was an ethics for 'free men', from which women, children and slaves were excluded. He rejects as a matter of principle the evocation of golden ages, and anyway the Ancient World was scarcely golden. But in a typically oblique manner, what he is doing in examining a time so different from our own is to throw our own needs and aspirations into relief. What we lack, he is suggesting, in not a transcendent truth, but ways of coping with a multiplicity of truths. We need not so much a morality based on absolute values, but an ethics (and politics I would add), for allowing us to cope with a variety of choices. Foucault, in taking us through the arts of existence in the ancient world, is asking us to reflect on the ways of life that could be valid for us today.

What would the basis of a modern sexual ethics be? There are hints in the distinction Foucault makes between freedom of 'sexual acts' and freedom of 'sexual choice'. He is against the first, he suggests, not least because it might involve endorsement of violent activity such as rape. It is also, of course, the mode of the sexual tradition. But he is for the second, whether it be, as he puts it 'the liberty to manifest that choice or not to manifest it' (Foucault 1982/83). The tenor of this is that the nature of the social relationships in which choice becomes meaningful is of crucial importance. We are being urged to move away from a situation where we judge the nature of the act, to one where we consider the context and the meaning of the act for the participants. I have already suggested some of the implications of this in the chapter on diversity. Here I want to look at the wider implications, for it points away from an absolutist morality, based on a fundamental human nature, to a fully pluralistic ethic, based on the acceptance of diverse tastes.

I have described this approach elsewhere as 'radical pluralism': pluralistic because it starts off with an assumption of the *fact* of diverse tastes, pleasures, and relationships; radical because of the positive endorsement of variety as a necessary accompaniment of our increasingly complex world (Weeks 1995). Rubin has argued that despite all the very real changes that have occurred:

> This culture always treats sex with suspicion. It construes and judges any sexual practice in terms of its worst possible expression. Sex is presumed guilty until proven innocent.
>
> (Rubin 1984: 278)

Moral pluralism begins with a different belief: that sex in itself is neither good nor bad, but is rather a field of possibilities and potentialities, all of which must be judged by the context in which they occur. It opens the way then, to acceptance of diversity as the *norm* of our culture and the appropriate means of thinking about sexuality.

This does not, of course, still all difficulties: in many ways, in fact, it compounds them. It is far easier to confront each difficult area of choice with a moral code which tells us exactly, and invariably, how we should live. In a social climate of rapid social – and moral – change, and of the emergence of new social possibilities, identities and lifestyles, it is a temptation to seek once again the security of absolute moral standards, which fixes us in a world of certainty where personal and social identities are given. Moral absolutism, as Alvin Gouldner has observed, 'serves to cut the Gordian knot of indecision', magically sweeping away doubt and anxiety and making possible the onward march of the army of the just (Gouldner 1973: 295). The radical pluralist approach, in sharp distinction to the absolutist tradition, is tentative, provisional and open-ended. It can be seen as partaking of some of the elements of the libertarian tradition – especially what may be called its 'sex-positive' attitudes – while at the same time it shares with the liberal tradition a recognition of the need for careful distinctions, for a grasp of meaning and context, and of the importance of the discourse of rights and choice. Where it differs from both these traditions is in its decisive recognition of the social production of sexualities, and their complex embeddedness in diverse power relations. Its aim, consequently, is to provide guidelines for decision making rather than new absolute values. It rejects the temptation of a 'radical morality'. Instead it places its emphasis on the merits of choice, and the conditions which limit choice.

Choice implies, in the first place, democracy. 'Democracy' may seem an odd word to apply to the sexual sphere, but it is surely a new concept of democracy that is called for when we speak of the right to control our bodies, when we say 'our bodies are our own'. The claim to bodily self-determination is an old one, with roots in a number of different moral and political traditions. From liberal roots in the puritan revolution of the seventeenth century we can trace the evolution of the idea of 'property in one's own person'. The Marxist tradition offers a vision of society in which human needs may be satisfied harmoniously. From the biological sciences comes the understanding of the body, its capacities and limitations, establishing the boundaries of individual possibility. All three of these recognize limits to the free exercise of bodily self-determination: through traditional, patriarchal authority, the unequal distribution of property and power, or the limits of the personality itself, with its needs for physical sustenance, emotional warmth, and above all, social involvement. From feminism has come a recognition of further limitations, the subtle and not so subtle coercions of a male-dominated society and the infiltration of inequality through all the relations of social life. Coward has argued:

> When we hear talk of freedom to choose sexual partners, we can be sure we'll also hear talk of visual appeal, the mysterious alchemy which strikes from the blue at the most awkward moments. And here's the coercion. Because women are compelled to make themselves attractive in certain ways, and those ways involve submitting to the culture's beliefs about appropriate sexual behaviour, women's appearances are laden down with cultural values, and women have to form their identities within these values, or, with difficulty, against them.
>
> (Coward 1984: 78)

A 'democratic morality', it has been suggested, would judge acts by the way partners deal with one another, the consideration they show for each other, the absence of coercion and the ability to negotiate equally and freely, their openness to one another, and the degree of pleasure and need they can satisfy [1]. These are admirable goals, but their recognition can be constantly thwarted by an awareness of the constraints that limit free choice.

There are real limitations in the society we live in to the free play of choice. But there is another issue which looms whenever the question of choice is raised: where should choice end? Should people be free, for instance, to choose activities that may harm themselves or others, whether intentionally or not? The problem here is not so much one of physical harm – which can be measured – but of psychic or moral damage – which usually cannot. Should, say, a just society ban pornography because of its exploitative representations of women? Should sado-masochistic sex be tolerated even between, in the famous phrase, 'consenting adults in private'? Harm is, of course, a difficult word to start with. Havelock Ellis in the 1930s, in what was to become a classical liberal formulation of the issue, believed that it was such a difficult concept that condemnation or interference could only be called for in two cases: if the subjects were in danger of damaging their health, and therefore likely to call on medical or psychotherapeutic treatment; or if there was a danger of injury to the health or rights of others, in which case the law was entitled to interfere (Ellis 1946: 184). These are, on the surface at least, very sensible guidelines, but they ignore a factor that has assumed a growing importance in recent debates on sexuality, a belief that 'damage' or 'harm' can be moral as well as physical, emotional as well as psychological. The hostility of some feminists to pornography and sado-masochistic activities relies on the argument that representations of violence can cause violence, and that sexual behaviour which flirts with power imbalances can sustain existing power relations.

The most powerful argument against this, also advanced by feminists, though of a rather different persuasion, is that attempts to suppress potentially harmful representations or fantasies do not in practice eliminate them but on the contrary reinforce their transgressive power. Jessica Benjamin has argued that our culture is facing a crisis of what she describes as 'male rationality', and a resurgence of erotic fantasy. She goes on:

> A politics that denies these issues, that tries to sanitize or rationalizes the erotic, fantastic components of human life, will not defeat domination, but only vacate the field.
>
> (Benjamin 1984: 308)

This, she believes, means the avoidance both of a simple libertarian acceptance and of moral condemnation [2]. The primary task is to understand. And what should the basis of our understanding be? Surely it must be a recognition that the complex forces that shape our sexualities – biological potentialities, unconscious motivations and desires, and social organization – produce many needs and wishes which often go beyond our dispassionate understanding or the canons of political correctness. Sexual excitement, Lynne Segal writes, 'is generated by, and in the service of, a multitude of needs, not all of them "nice"' (Segal 1983: 45). This implies, rightly in my opinion, that sexuality is too difficult and elusive an idea to be tidied away into neat compartments of right or wrong. We need to be alive to its ambivalent and ambiguous qualities, and act accordingly.

Sexual 'choice', then, suggests a recognition of limits as well as possibilities, hazardous paths as much as positive goals. It must also, however, take into account another reality: the fact of conflicting choices, opposed goals. As I have already noted the debate on abortion has produced ultimately irreconcilable 'rights': those of the 'unborn child' against those of the mother who claims a right to control her own fertility. Here there are massively different conceptions in conflict: different views of what constitutes 'life', and opposing claims over the absolute autonomy of the body. But even within the broad parameters of a common social and political affiliation the 'right to choose' can have different meanings in different contexts. The feminist claim to a right to choose abortion must also involve a right to choose *not* to have an abortion. In societies where marginalized and poor women may be encouraged (either for racist and/or population policy reasons) to limit their family size, a call for the right to abortion will appear narrowly exclusive. This has led to a shift amongst feminists away from a campaign simply for abortion rights to a wider campaign to ensure 'reproductive rights' for women as a whole – to embrace campaigns against compulsory sterilization or compulsory abortion as well as for full access to effective birth control and the rights of women to terminate their pregnancies, if they choose [3].

The context in which choice is demanded and operative is, therefore, critical. Sexual values cannot be detached from the wider social values we hold, and these themselves are increasingly diverse. We saw earlier that the world of sexuality is fragmented by a number of other relations: of race, gender and class particularly. This means that different groups will endorse different perspectives and develop often strikingly opposed priorities. The white feminist critique of the family, for example, may appear ethnocentric and oppressive to black feminists struggling to defend their families against racist immigration procedures which may work to split families. Similarly, the priority given by gay and lesbian movements to 'coming out', to openly declaring your sexual preferences as a means of affirming their validity, often conflicts with the need felt by black lesbians and gay men in a racist culture to affirm their political identity with their communities of origin, whatever the family and sexual orthodoxies prevailing there (Amos and Parmar 1984; Ormodale 1984). A discourse of choice must therefore be based not only on a recognition of different individual needs and goals, but of different means of living them.

There is another important factor that needs to be stressed. The priority given to diversity and choice runs the danger of appearing as a purely individual activity, with each isolated monad having to make his or her choice in the face of a multitude of options. This supermarket view of sex is in many ways complicit with the vast changes that have reshaped the globe since the 1980s, leading as some commentators have argued to the 'postmodernization of sex' (Simon 1996: ch. 1). We seem to live in a world of glittering flux, where we have no choice but to choose, perhaps, but often find it impossible to make up our minds. The individual may seem thrown back on his or her own resources, and many individuals, as we know, flail around in an apparently meaningless void in such situations. The lessons of the history of sexual politics suggest, however, that it is mutuality, a sense of our continuing and necessary involvement with others, that ultimately provides the real guarantee of individual choice and of meaningfulness (Weeks 1995). The new patterns of intimacy that I discussed in the previous chapter do not presage a decline of reciprocity, but its reinvention, where individual needs and mutual commitments are negotiated in a post-traditional world. More broadly, the apparent triumph of individualization in the late modern world may signal the decline of old solidarities, but it would be foolish to ignore the simultaneous rise of new possibilities. The emergence of new political subjects – feminists, lesbians and gays, and other sexual minorities alongside many other social movements – has dramatized the changes that are taking place in the political ecology of the West, with often profound effects on the workings of its representative systems. But more crucially for this discussion, they have demonstratively made possible the new individual self-assertion of women, homosexuals and others that has changed the sexual scene of the West. The new vocabulary of sexual needs and desires is overwhelmingly a product of what can best be called 'collective self-activity'.

This is the point where sexual politics inevitably returns to its wider social context, and its moral and political alignments. The choices we are confronted with are decided in the end not by anything intrinsic to sexuality itself but by the wider set of values and goals which we embrace. This brings us back to the ideal of democracy. A sexual democracy necessarily implies a wider process of democratization in which the barriers that restrict individual potentiality and growth – the barriers of economic exploitations and class divisions, racial oppressions and gender inequalities, moral authoritarianism and educational disadvantage, poverty and insecurity – are progressively dismantled. This must not be taken to imply that real difficulties, real divisions of need and interest, real conflicts of priority or of desire, will, or ought to, disappear. The aim, on the contrary, ought to be to maximize the means by which these differences and conflicts can be resolved democratically.

As society becomes ever more complex it is likely that the patterns of individual sexual needs and relationships will be in ever more exotic flux. I have suggested in this essay that we should be more ready than we have been to go with the flood: to fully accept the possibilities opened up by a growing social and moral pluralism, to embrace, in all their accompanying ambiguities and potential conflicts, the merits of sexual diversity and choice. The sexual tradition offered a fundamentally monolithic construct which we know as 'sexuality'. In recent years its pretensions have been punctured, its dubious origins revealed and its restrictive effects exposed. We have deconstructed the idea of sexuality. It is now time to start thinking afresh about individual needs and aspirations, and the social policies that can satisfy them; to think about the proper balance between private pleasures and public policies. A genuine acceptance of moral pluralism seems the only appropriate starting point.

[handwritten marginalia]: have stud's in gps discuss their sexual ethics - the 3 options he mentions p 105 absolutist/ libertarian, lib-pluralist

SUGGESTIONS FOR FURTHER READING

The first edition of this book appeared whilst the serious study of the history and social organization of sexuality was still developing. Today it has become a vast scholarly industry, and no short book can hope to cover all aspects of the field. Suggestions for further reading can barely hint at the current richness of the literature. What follows is therefore selective, but will, I hope, provide the opening to a fuller exploration.

Let me begin with my own writings, if for no other reason than that the reader is entitled to know where I am coming from. The perspective outlined in this essay is elaborated in greater detail in a number of books I have written on the social organization of sexuality. These include: Jeffrey Weeks, *Coming Out. Homosexual Politics in Britain from the 19th Century to the Present*, Quartet, London (1977; 2nd edition 1990); *Sex, Politics and Society. The Regulation of Sexuality since 1800*, Longman, Harlow (1981; 2nd edition 1989); *Sexuality and its Discontents. Meanings, Myths and Modern Sexualities*, Routledge & Kegan Paul, London (1985); *Against Nature: Essays on History, Sexuality and Identity*, Rivers Oram Press, London (1991); *Invented Moralities: Sexual Values in an Age of Uncertainty*, Polity Press, Cambridge (1995); *Sexual Cultures: Communities, Values and Intimacy*, edited with Janet Holland, Macmillan, Basingstoke (1996); *Making Sexual History*, Polity Press, Cambridge (2000); and *Same Sex Intimacies: Families of Choice and other Life Experiments*, with Brian Heaphy and Catherine Donovan, Routledge, London and New York (2001). These all contain detailed notes and references which may be pursued for further reading.

My own writings have been informed by personal and collective research but also owe immense debts to the scholarship of many others. There are now a number of excellent collections which bring together the fruits of some of the best of this contemporary scholarship. The outstanding work is the four volume collection of papers edited by Ken Plummer: *Sexualities, Vol. I, Making a Sociology of Sexualities; Vol. II, Some Elements for an Account of the Social Organization of Sexualities; Vol. III, Difference and the Diversity of Sexualities; Vol. IV, Sexualities and their Futures*, Critical Concepts in Sociology, Routledge, London and New York (2002). Plummer's collection attempts to cover the whole range of writings on the sociology of sexuality. A shorter collection, concentrating on the best of recent writings on the history, sociology and politics of sexuality, is my own selection, made with colleagues: Jeffrey Weeks, Janet Holland and Matthew Waites (eds), *Sexualities and Society: A Reader*, Polity Press, Cambridge (2003). I would also recommend the following collections, their organizing theme suggested by their titles: Richard Parker and Peter Aggleton (eds), *Culture, Society and Sexuality: A Reader*, UCL Press, London (1999); Richard Parker, Marie Barbosa and Peter Aggleton, *Framing the Sexual Subject: The Politics of Gender, Sexuality and Power*, University of California Press, Berkeley, Los Angeles and London (2000); Kim M. Phillips and Barry Reay (eds), *Sexualities in History: A Reader*, Routledge, New York and London (2002); Christine Williams and Arlene Stein (eds), *Sexuality and Gender*, Blackwell, Oxford (2002); and Robert Hearley and Betsy Crane (eds), *Sexual Lives: A Reader on the Theories and Realities of Human Sexualities*, McGraw Hill, New York (2003).

A number of specialist journals now exist which provide ample opportunities to explore the various aspects of sexuality. I want especially to mention three journals which publish important articles relevant to the arguments in this book: *Sexualities*; *Journal of the History of Sexuality*; and *Culture, Health and Sexuality*.

The history of the study of sexuality, sexology, has rightfully become a key theme, because it illustrates that the ways in which we write about sexuality to a large extent set the parameters by which we can live it. The Viennese psychiatrist Richard von Krafft-Ebing was in a very real sense the Founding Father of sexology. An outstanding study of his work and influence has been written by Harry Oosterhuis: *Stepchildren of Nature: Krafft-Ebing, Psychiatry and the Making of Sexual Identity*, University of Chicago Press, Chicago and London (2000). For the context in which he was writing, see Roy Porter and Mikulas Teich (eds), *Sexual Knowledge, Sexual Science: The History of Attitudes to Sexuality*, Cambridge University Press, Cambridge (1994); and two volumes edited by Lucy Bland and Laura Doan: *Sexology in Culture: Labelling Bodies and Desires*; and *Sexology Uncensored: The Documents of Sexual Science*, both Polity Press, Cambridge (1998).

For psychoanalysis, the starting point should be Sigmund Freud himself, especially *Three Essays on the Theory of Sexuality*, first published in 1905 and much revised over the next 20 years. It is available in Volume 7 of *The Standard Edition of the Complete Psychological Works of Sigmund Freud* edited by James Strachey, Hogarth Press and the Institute of Psychoanalysis, London (1953). In Britain it is available in paperback in Volume 7 of The Pelican Freud Library, *On Sexuality*, Penguin, Harmondsworth (1977), together with other useful papers. Discussions of the significance of Freud to contemporary analyses of sexuality can be found in: Juliet Mitchell, *Psychoanalysis and Feminism*, Allen Lane, London (1973); Rosalind Coward, *Patriarchal Precedents. Sexuality and Social Relations*, Routledge & Kegan

Paul, London (1983); *Female Desire. Women's Sexuality Today*, Paladin, London (1984); Jacques Lacan and the Ecole Freudienne, *Feminine Sexuality*, edited by Juliet Mitchell and Jacqueline Rose, Macmillan, London (1982); Teresa de Lauretis, *Practice of Love: Lesbian Sexuality and Perverse Desire*, Indiana University Press, Bloomington and Indianopolis (1994); and Celia Harding (ed.), *Sexuality: Psychoanalytic Perspectives*, Brunner and Routledge, Hove (2001). For some excellent short essays on psychoanalysis and sexuality, see Elizabeth Wright (ed.), *Feminism and Psychoanalysis: A Critical Dictionary*, Blackwell, Oxford (1992).

Recent sociological debates on sexuality can be followed in the four volumes edited by Plummer, cited above. Major sociological contributions, especially from within the interactionist tradition, which have influenced my own thinking, include: John H. Gagnon and William Simon, *Sexual Conduct. The Social Sources of Human Sexuality*, Hutchinson, London (1973); John H. Gagnon, *Human Sexualities*, Scott, Foresman and Co., Glenview, Illinois (1977); Kenneth Plummer, *Sexual Stigma. An Interactionist Account*, Routledge & Kegan Paul, London (1975); Ken Plummer, *Telling Sexual Stories: Power, Change and Social Worlds*, Routledge, London and New York (1995); and William Simon, *Postmodern Sexualities*, Routledge, London and New York (1994). For other recent critical sociological accounts of sexuality see Gail Hawkes, *A Sociology of Sex and Sexuality*, Open University Press, Buckingham and Philadelphia (1996); Diane Richardson, *Rethinking Sexuality*, Sage, London and Thousand Oaks (2000); and Lisa Adkins, *Revisions: Gender and Sexuality in Late Modernity*, Open University Press, Buckingham (2002).

No contemporary writer on sexuality can escape the influence of Michel Foucault, even if the end result is a total rejection of his works. His views are polemically summed up in *The History of Sexuality, Vol. 1, An Introduction*, Allen Lane, London (1979). The two posthumous volumes were originally published as Michel Foucault, *Histoire de la sexualite: 2, L'Usage des plaisirs; 3, Le Souci de soi*, Editions Gallimard, Paris (1984); translated as *The History of Sexuality, Vol. 2, The Use of Pleasure*, Viking, London (1985); and *The History of Sexuality, Vol. 3, The Care of the Self*, Viking, London (1986).

Foucault's interviews often provide many clarifying insights concerning his overall project. See especially *Power/Knowledge: Selected Interviews and Other Writings 1972–1977*, edited by Colin Gordon, Harvester Press, Brighton (1980); *The Foucault Reader,* edited by Paul Rabinow, Pantheon Books, New York (1984); and J. Bernauer and D. Rasmussen (eds), *The Final Foucault*, MIT Press, Cambridge, Mass. (1988). Although no substitute for reading the originals, there is a vast corpus of commentaries on

Foucault. I recommend two of high, if differing quality: Lois McNay, *Foucault: A Critical Introduction*, Polity Press, Cambridge (1994); and David M. Halperin, *Saint Foucault: Towards a Gay Hagiography*, Oxford University Press, Oxford and New York (1995).

The feminist contribution to sexual theory and practice has been critical. Stevi Jackson and Sue Scott bring together many of the most important contributions in their edited volume *Feminism and Sexuality: A Reader*, Edinburgh University Press, Ediburgh (1996). Two earlier and highly influential collections of articles, which were themselves interventions in the feminist debates on sexuality, contain a wide range of material on the theory, history, sociology, poetry and politics (especially feminist politics) of sex: Ann Snitow, Christine Stansell and Sharon Thompson (eds), *Desire. The Politics of Sexuality*, Virago, London (1983), published in the USA as: *Powers of Desire: The Politics of Sexuality*, Monthly Review Press, New York (1983); and Carole S. Vance (ed.), *Pleasure and Danger. Exploring Female Sexuality*, Routledge & Kegan Paul, London and Boston (1984). A long essay in the latter by Gayle Rubin, 'Thinking sex: notes for a radical theory of the politics of sexuality' is particularly important, and has been widely anthologized. Both these volumes contain useful articles about the interconnections between race and sexuality. The shaping of gender and the 'invention' of heterosexuality and homosexuality has become a major theme in the exploration of sexuality. Thomas Laqueur has traced the evolution of conceptualizations of the male and female bodies and sexualities in *Making Sex: Body and Gender from the Greeks to Freud*, Harvard University Press, Cambridge, Mass., and London (1990). His latest contribution also provides a broad history of sexuality as well as a detailed history of its ostensible subject: *Solitary Sex: A Cultural History of Masturbation*, Zone Books, New York and London (2003). A helpful, if variable, survey of Western attitudes to sex can be found in: Philippe Aries and Andre Bejin (eds), *Western Sexuality, Practice and Precept in Past and Present Times*, Basil Blackwell, Oxford (1985). Lawrence Stone's massive, *The Family, Sex and Marriage in England* 1500–1800, Weidenfeld & Nicolson, London (1977), provides an overview of (chiefly upper class) attitudes for the period. Randolph Trumbach has explored the 'gender revolution' of the eighteenth century in *Sex and the Gender Revolution, Volume One: Heterosexuality and the Third Gender in Enlightenment London*, University of Chicago Press, Chicago and London (1998). An entertaining and insightful account of the concept of heterosexuality has been written by Jonathan Ned Katz, *The Invention of Heterosexuality*, Dutton, New York (1995).

Barbara Ehrenreich has explored male fears of commitment in what has become a classic: *The Hearts of Men. American Dreams and the Flight from*

Commitment, Pluto, London (1983), first published by Anchor Press/ Doubleday, New York (1983). The conflict between duty and desire amongst feminists is explored in a pioneering collection: Sue Cartledge and Joanna Ryan (eds), *Sex and Love. New Thoughts on Old Contradictions,* The Women's Press, London (1983). For valuable essays from within the the feminist debate on heterosexuality, see Diane Richardson (ed.),*Theorising Heterosexuality: Telling it Straight,* Open University Press, Buckingham and Philadelphia (1996); Stevi Jackson. *Heterosexuality in Question,* Sage, London (2000). See also Lynne Segal, *Straight Sex: The Politics of Pleasure,* Virago, London (1994); Janet Holland, Caroline Ramazanoglu, Sue Sharpe and Rachel Thomson, *The Male in the Head,* The Tufnell Press, London (1998). Detailed examples of the institutionalization of heterosexuality can be found in Janet Holland and Lisa Adkins (eds), *Sex, Sensibility and the Gendered Body,* Macmillan, Basingstoke (1996); Lisa Adkins and Vicki Merchant (eds), *Sexualizing the Social: Power and the Organization of Sexuality,* Macmillan, Basingstoke (1996); Lisa Adkins, *Gendered Work: Sexuality, Family and the Labour Market,* Open University Press, Buckingham (1995); Jeff Hearn, Deborah L. Sheppard, Peta Tancred-Sheriff and Gibson Burrell (eds), *The Sexuality of Organization,* Sage, London, Newbury Park and New Delhi (1989). The impact of sexual violence in sustaining male domination is explored in the pioneering book by Elizabeth Wilson, *What is to be Done about Violence against Women?,* Penguin, Harmondsworth (1983); and in Jeff Hearn and Wendy Parkin, *Gender, Sexuality and Violence in Organizations: Unspoken Forces of Gender, Sexuality, Violence and Violation in Organizational Worlds,* Sage, London and Beverley Hills (2001): and Barbara Fawcett, Brid Featherstone, Jeff Hearn and Christine Toft (eds), *Violence and Gender Relations: Theories and Interventions,* Sage, London and Beverley Hills (1996). R. W. Connell has produced classic studies of gender, power and masculinity. See particularly his *Gender and Power,* Polity Press, Cambridge (1987); *Masculinities,* Polity Press, Cambridge (1995); and *Gender,* Polity Press, Cambridge (2002).

A vast and ever-growing literature on the history, sociology, politics and culture of homosexuality provides major insights into the 'invention of sexuality' in general, and the construction of same-sex desire in particular. The range of the debates can be seen in Peter M. Nardi and Beth E. Schneider (eds), *Sexual Perspectives in Lesbian and Gay Studies: A Reader,* Routledge, London and New York (1998); Theo Sandfort, Judith Schuyf, Jan Willem Duyvendak and Jeffrey Weeks (eds), *Lesbian and Gay Studies: An Introductory, Interdisciplinary Approach,* Sage, London, Thousand Oaks and New Delhi (2000); Steven Seidman (ed.), *Queer Theory/Sociology,* Blackwell,

Oxford (1996); and Diane Richardson and Steven Seidman (eds), *Handbook of Lesbian and Gay Studies*, Sage, London, Thousand Oaks and New Delhi (2002). The 'essentialist/constructionist' controversy can be traced in Edward Stein (ed.), *Forms of Desire: Sexual Orientation and the Social Constructionist Controversy*, Routledge, New York and London (1992).

For major scholarly contributions on the evolution of same-sex desires and identities, see John Boswell, *Social Tolerance and Homosexuality. Gay People in Western Europe from the Beginning of the Christian Era to the Fourteenth Century*, University of Chicago Press, Chicago and London (1980); John Boswell, *Same Sex Unions in Pre-modern Europe*, Villard Books, New York (1994); Alan Bray, *Homosexuality in Renaissance England*, Gay Men's Press, London (1982); Jonathan Ned Katz, *Gay/Lesbian Almanac*, Harper & Row, New York (1983); Jonathan Ned Katz, *Love Stories: Sex Between Men before Homosexuality*, University of Chicago Press, Chicago (2001); Lillian Faderman, *Surpassing the Love of Men. Romantic Friendship and Love between Women from the Renaissance to the Present*, Junction Books, London (1980); Kenneth Plummer (ed.), *The Making of the Modern Homosexual*, Hutchinson, London (1981), and *Modern Homosexualities, Fragments of Lesbian and Gay Experience*, Routledge, London and New York (1992); Estelle B. Freedman *et al.*, *The Lesbian Issue. Essays from Signs*, University of Chicago Press, Chicago and London (1985); Martha Vicinus (ed.), *Lesbian Subjects: A Feminist Review Reader*, Indiana University Press, Bloomington and Indianopolis (1996); and *Sexualities* Vol. 3, No. 2, May 2000: Special Issue: 'Speaking from a Lesbian Position: Opening up Sexual Studies'.

For homosexuality in a range of cross-cultural contexts, both historical and contemporary, see Rudi C. Bleys, *The Geography of Perversion: Male-to-male Sexual Behaviour outside the West and the Ethnographic Imagination, 1750–1918*, Cassell, London (1996); George Chauncey, *Gay New York: Gender, Urban Culture, and the Making of the Gay Male World*, Basic Books, New York (1994); Gary W. Dowsett, *Practicing Desire: Homosexual Sex in the Era of AIDS*, Stanford University Press, Stanford, Ca. (1996); David M. Halperin, *One Hundred Years of Homosexuality. And Other Essays on Greek Love*, Routledge, London and New York (1990), and *How to Do the History of Homosexuality*, University of Chicago Press, Chicago (2002); Gilbert Herdt, *Third Sex, Third Gender: Beyond Sexual Dimorphism in Culture and History*, Zone Books, New York (1994); Richard G. Parker, *Bodies, Pleasures and Passions: Sexual Culture in Contemporary Brazil*, Beacon Press, Boston (1991), and *Beneath the Equator: Cultures of Desire, Male Homosexuality and Emerging Gay Communities in Brazil*, Routledge, London and New York (1999); Stephen O. Murray, *Homosexualities*, University of Chicago Press, Chicago (2000); Robert Reynolds, *From Camp to Queer: Remaking the*

Australian Homosexual, Melbourne University Press, Melbourne (2002); Steven Seidman, *Beyond the Closet: The Transformation of Gay and Lesbian Life*, Routledge, New York and London (2002); and Tamsin Wilton, *Unexpected Pleasures: Leaving Heterosexuality for a Lesbian Life*, Diva Ltd, London (2003). A global overview is provided in Barry D. Adam, Jan Willem Duyvendak and Andre Krouwel, *The Global Emergence of Lesbian and Gay Politics*, Temple University Press, Philadelphia (1996).

For the 'queer' critique (though not all the following accept that label) see Michael Warner (ed.), *Fear of a Queer Planet: Queer Politics and Social Theory*, University of Minnesota Press, Minneapolis and London (1993); Jonathan Dollimore, *Sexual Dissidence: Augustine to Wilde, Freud to Foucault*, Clarendon Press, Oxford (1991); Judith Butler, *Gender Trouble: Feminism and the Subversion of Identity*, Routledge, New York and London (1990); Judith Butler, *Bodies that Matter: On the Discursive Limits of Sex*, Routledge, New York and London (1993). See also Robert J. Corber and Stephen Valocchi (eds), *Queer Studies: An Interdisciplinary Reader*, Blackwell, Malden, Mass., and Melbourne (2003).

On the biology and psychology of sexual differences, see John Nicholson, *Men and Women. How Different are They*, Oxford University Press, Oxford and New York (1984); Ann Oakley, *Sex, Gender and Society* (revised edition), Gower, Aldershot (1985). Brian Sykes, *Adams's Curse*, Bantam, New York (2003), argues that men are an endangered species. Evolutionary psychology positions are advanced in Simon Baron-Cohen, *The Essential Difference: Men, Women, and the Extreme Male Brain*, Allen Lane, London (2003); and Matt Ridley, *Nature via Nurture*, Fourth Estate, London (2003). For critiques of such positions, see Steven Rose, Leon J. Kamin and R. C. Lewontin, *Not in our Genes. Biology, Ideology and Human Nature*, Penguin Harmondsworth (1984); Julian Henriques *et al.*, *Changing the Subject. Psychology, Social Regulation and Subjectivity*, Methuen, London and New York (1984); Hilary Rose and Steven Rose (eds), *Alas, Poor Darwin: Arguments against Evolutionary Psychology*, Vintage Books, London (2001); Lynne Segal, *Why Feminism?*, Polity Press, Cambridge (1999); Steve Jones, *Y: The Descent of Men*, Little, Brown, London (2002); and Roger. N. Lancaster, *The Trouble with Nature: Sex in Science and Popular Culture*, University of California Press (2003). Timothy Taylor has produced an engaging overview of the origins and development of sex in *The Prehistory of Sex: Four Million Years of Human Sexual Culture*, Fourth Estate, London (1996). A brilliant and readable overview of the contribution of genetics to our understanding of human history can be found in Luigi Luca Cavalli-Sforza, *Genes, Peoples and Language*, Allen Lane, The Penguin Press, London (2000).

Discussions of the meaning of 'sexual perversion' can be found in Robert J. Stoller, *Perversion. The Erotic Form of Hatred*, Quartet, London (1977); Janine Chasseguet-Smirgel, *Creativity and Perversion*, Free Association Books, London (1985); and the essays in K. Howells (ed.), *Sexual Diversity*, Blackwell, Oxford (1984). Debates on SM can be traced in Bill Thompson, *Sadomasochism: Painful Perversion or Pleasurable Play?*, Cassell, London (1994). Controversies over child abuse are discussed in Paula Reavey and Sam Warner (eds), *New Feminist Stories of Child Sexual Abuse: Sexual Scripts and Dangerous Dialogues*, Routledge, London and New York (2003). For bisexualities, see Merl Storr (ed.), *Bisexuality: A Critical Reader* Routledge, London and New York (1999); and Marjorie Garber, *Vice Versa: Bisexuality and the Eroticism of Everyday Life*, Hamish Hamilton, London (1995). On transgender, see Marjorie Garber again, *Vested Interests: Cross Dressing and Cultural Anxiety*, Routledge, New York and London (1992); Kate More and Stephen Whittle (eds), *Reclaiming Genders: Transsexual Grammar and the Fin de Siècle*, Cassell, London (1999); and Richard Ekins and Dave King (eds), *Blending Genders: Social Aspects of Cross-dressing and Sex-changing*, Routledge, London and New York (1996).

The importance of the spatial organization of eroticism and sexual identities are discussed in David Bell and Gill Valentine (eds), *Mapping Desire*, Routledge, London and New York (1995); Gill Valentine, 'Queer Bodies and the Production of Space', in Richardson and Seidman (eds), cited above; Gordon Brent Ingram, Anne-Marie Bouthillette and Yolanda Retter (eds), *Queers in Space: Communities, Public Spaces, Sites of Resistance*, Bay Press, Seattle (1997); William L. Leap (ed.), *Public Sex, Gay Space*, Columbia University Press, New York (1999).

There is now a vast literature on HIV/AIDS. For a pioneering study which captures the initial reactions in the USA, see Dennis Altman, *AIDS and the Mind of America*, New York, Doubleday (1986), published in Britain as *AIDS and the New Puritans* Pluto, London (1986); see also Altman's *Power and Community: Organizational and Cultural Responses to AIDS*, Taylor and Francis, London and Bristol, Pa. (1994). The historical framing of the epidemic is examined in Elizabeth Fee and Danile M. Fox (eds), *AIDS: the Burdens of History*, University of California Press, Berkeley (1988) and (by the same authors) *AIDS: the Making of a Chronic Disease*, University of California Press, Berkeley (1992). Steven Epstein has produced a powerful analysis of the interface been AIDS activism and the construction of knowledge about HIV/AIDS in *Pure Science: AIDS, Activism and the Politics of Knowledge*, University of Californian Press, Berkeley, Los Angeles and London (1996). For the international dimensions of the epidemic, see Mary Haour-Knipe and Richard Rector (eds), *Crossing Borders: Migrations,*

Ethnicity and AIDS, Taylor and Francis, London and Bristol, Pa. (1996); and Jean-Paul Moatti, Yves Souteyrand, Annice Prieur, Theo Sandfort and Peter Aggleton, *AIDS in Europe: New Challenges for the Social Sciences*, Routledge, London and New York (2000). For a national study which illuminates many of the key issues, see Philip Gatter, *Identity and Sexuality: AIDS in Britain in the 1990s*, Cassell, London (1999). Simon Watney is a master of passionate engagement and polemic concerning the epidemic. See his *Imagine Hope: AIDS and Gay Identity*, Routledge, London and New York (2000). On the gendering of the epidemic, see Tamsin Wilton, *En-gendering AIDS: Deconstructing Sex, Text, Epidemic*, Sage, London, Thousand Oaks and New Delhi (1997). The HIV/AIDS epidemic is multifaceted and rapidly changing. For up-to-date information, see the website of UNAIDS, the global response to the epidemic: www.unaids.org/

The fraught politics of sexuality since the 1960s is a subject in its own right. For the basic data on sexual attitudes, see Edward O. Laumann, Robert T. Michael, John H. Gagnon and S. Michaels, *The Social Organization of Sexuality: Sexual Practices in the United States*, University of Chicago Press, Chicago (1994); Kaye Wellings, Julia Field, Anne M. Johnson and J. Wadsworth, *Sexual Behaviour in Britain: The National Survey of Sexual Attitudes and Lifestyles*, Macmillan, London and Basingstoke (1994); Anne M. Johnson, Catherine H. Mercer, Bob Erens *et al.*, 'Sexual behaviour in Britain: partnerships, practices, and HIV risk behaviours', *The Lancet*, Vol. 358 (9296), 1 December 2001, pp. 1835–42. For the links between the politics of nationalism and the politics of sexuality, see Andrew Parker, Mary Russo, Doris Sommer and Patricia Yaegar (eds), *Nationalism and Sexualities*, Routledge, New York and London (1992). Useful essays can be found in Terrell Carver and Veronique Mottier (eds), *Politics of Sexuality: Identity, Gender, Citizenship*, Routledge, London and New York (1998). On the New Right, see Anne Marie Smith, *New Right Discourses on Race and Sexuality. Britain 1968–1990*, Cambridge University Press, Cambridge (1994); Didi Herman, *The Anti Gay Agenda: Orthodox Vision and the Christian Right*, University of Chicago Press, Chicago (1997); and Amy Ansell (ed.), *Unraveling the Right: The New Conservatism in American Thought and Politics*, Westview Press, Boulder, Co. (2001). The impact of the debate on pornography, amongst other things, in sexual politics can be traced in Lisa Duggan and Nan D. Hunter, *Sex Wars: Sexual Dissent and Political Culture*, Routledge, New York and London (1995); and in Bill Thompson, *Soft Core: Moral Crusades against Pornography in Britain and America*, Cassell, London (1994).

Sexual or intimate citizenship has become a key theme in contemporary discussions of sexuality. The pioneering study was David Evans, *Sexual*

Citizenship: The Material Construction of Sexualities, Routledge, London and New York (1985). For subsequent studies, see David Bell and Jon Binnie, *The Sexual Citizen: Queer Politics and Beyond*, Polity Press, Cambridge (2000); Shane Phelan, *Sexual Strangers: Gays, Lesbians, and Dilemmas of Citizenship*, Temple University Press, Philadelphia (2001); Ken Plummer, 'The Square of Intimate Citizenship', *Citizenship Studies*, Vol. 5, No. 3, November 2002, pp. 237–53; and Plummer, *Inventing Intimate Citizenship*, University of Washington Press, Seattle (2003). My own contribution to the debate can be found in 'The Sexual Citizen', *Theory, Culture and Society*, Vol. 15, Nos 3–4, 1998, pp. 35–52.

Changes in patterns of intimacy are crucial to understanding contemporary patterns of sexuality. See especially Anthony Giddens, *The Transformation of Intimacy: Sexuality, Love and Eroticism in Modern Societies*, Polity Press, Cambridge (1992); Lynn Jamieson, *Intimacy: Personal Relationships in Modern Societies*, Polity Press, Cambridge (1998); and in Holland *et al.*, *The Male in the Head*; and Weeks *et al.*, *Same Sex Intimacies*, both cited above. The new globalized context of contemporary intimacies and sexualities is discussed in Dennis Altman, *Global Sex*, University of Chicago Press, Chicago (2001); Bonnie G. Smith (ed.), *Global Feminisms since 1945: Rewriting Histories*, Routledge, New York and London (2000); and the related impact of the internet is discussed in Jenny Wolmark (ed.), *Cybersexualities: A Reader in Feminist Theory, Cyborgs and Cyberspace*, Edinburgh University Press, Edinburgh (1999).

Many of these publications capture a moment in the literature of sexuality, shaped by particular intellectual and political currents. This book itself is a product of many of those currents, and as the substantial revisions from the first edition illustrate, the debates are continuously evolving as the everyday realities of sexuality themselves change. The vibrancy of the debates perhaps illustrates above all the centrality that sexuality has assumed not only in our individual lives but in our collective experience. That is what the social and historical understanding of sexuality is ultimately concerned with.

Notes

1 THE LANGUAGES OF SEX

[1] The terms are discussed in Williams (1983: 283–6).
[2] For a variety of sociological and historical perspectives, see Weeks *et al.* (2003). On globalization see Altman (2001).

2 THE INVENTION OF SEXUALITY

[1] See Bullough (1976); the particular essay, 'Sex in history: a virgin field', was first published in 1972.
[2] See Dawkins (1978). I discuss sociobiology in Chapter 3.
[3] Padgug (1979). For contributions to the debate on sex in history, including Padgug's essay, as well as a contribution from myself, see Phillips and Reay (2002).
[4] Mead (1977; first published 1928). For a highly critical dissection of this work, see Freeman (1983).
[5] The phrase is used by Malinowski in 'Culture as a determinant of behavior' (reprinted in Malinowski 1963: 167).
[6] See Cartledge and Ryan (1983: 1). For an overview of the essentialist–constructionist controversy, see Stein (1992).
[7] Altman (1982). For a discussion of the impact of AIDS, see Chapter 5.
[8] See Ford and Beach (1965; first published 1952) and Kinsey *et al.,* (1953). Compare comments in Argyle and Henderson (1985: 159).
[9] For fuller details, see the discussion in Weeks (1989: ch. 4).
[10] See the discussion in Weeks (1985: 89–91 and ch. 8).
[11] See Coveney *et al.* (1984); and discussion in Jackson 2000.
[12] See the summary of evidence in Amos and Parmar (1984), Anthias and Yuval Davis (1983; 1993: 100–1).

3 THE MEANINGS OF SEXUAL DIFFERENCE

[1] See the discussion in Weeks (1985: 80–5).
[2] See Masters and Johnson (1966). On classical views of a single sex, see Laqueur (1990).
[3] Wilson (1978: 3); Thornhill and Palmer (2000). For a critique of these arguments, see Rose and Rose (2001), and Segal (1999: 78–115).
[4] Cherfas and Gribbin (1984: 178). But see Jones (2002).

[5] Bell *et al.* (1981: 191–2). On the gay gene/gay brain controversy, see Hamer *et al.* (1993), LeVay (1991) and Rose (1996).

[6] Archer and Lloyd (1982: 47–8). Ironically, Archer subsequently became an enthusiastic supporter of evolutionary psychology. See Archer and Lloyd 2002; and comments in Segal (1999: 87–8).

[7] Gagnon (1977: 6). For subsequent development of these ideas, see Plummer (1995) Simon (1994).

[8] Freud (1916–17: 210). For a fuller discussion of Freud's various theorizations of sexuality, see Weeks (1985: ch. 6).

[9] See particularly Mitchell (1974). For various critical takes on this position, see Rose (1986), Lauretis (1994) and Butler (1993).

[10] For broader discussions of masculinity, see Connell (1995, 2002).

4 THE CHALLENGE OF DIVERSITY

[1] Foucault (1979). On the role of the founding father of sexology, see Oosterhuis (2000).

[2] For a fuller discussion, see Weeks(1995).

[3] Bayer (1981). On similar moves in Australia, see Barr *et al.* (1984) and Reynolds (2002).

[4] For a cogent defence of feminist heterosexual practice, see Segal (1994).

[5] O'Carroll (1980: 153). For the various legitimations offered, see the discussion in Plummer (1981).

[6] There is an excellent debate on the implications of the early twenty-first century anxiety about paedophilia in Loseke *et al.* (2003). For feminist perspectives, see Reavey and Warner (2003).

[7] For a strong defence of SM, see Samois (1982); for an opposing view, see Linden *et al.* (1982). For an overview, see Thompson (1994).

5 SEXUALITY, INTIMACY AND POLITICS

[1] Speech of 27 March 1982.

[2] See the discussion in Weeks (1995; 2000).

[3] See chapters by, inter alia, Oliver Phillips and M. Jacqui Alexander in Weeks *et al.* (2003).

[4] For the changing patterns of behaviour and attitudes in the USA and the UK, see Laumann *et al.* (1994) and Wellings *et al.* (1994); and an update of the latter in Johnson *et al.* (2001).

[5] For a summary of reactions, see chapter 7 'AIDS and the Regulation of Sexuality' in Weeks (2000).

[6] For up-to-date information, see the website of UNAIDS, the global response to the epidemic: <www.unaids.org/>. For a powerful summary of the global dangers, see the article by Kofi Annan, Secretary-General of the United Nations (Annan 2003).

[7] This 'gnostic' approach is discussed in Davis (1983). For more on trangression, see Dollimore (1991).

[8] For a broader discussion, see Weeks (1985).

[9] For an overview, see Petchesky and Judd (1998) and Altman 2001.

6 PRIVATE PLEASURES AND PUBLIC POLICY

[1] See discussion in Giddens (1992: ch. 10) and Jamieson (1998: ch. 6).

[2] Benjamin (1984). For pertinent comments, see Segal (1998).

[3] See the discussion in Petchesky and Judd (1998).

BIBLIOGRAPHY

Adam, Barry (1978) *The Survival of Domination, Inferiorisation and Everyday Life,* Elsevier, New York, Oxford.

Adam, Barry (1995) *The Rise of a Lesbian and Gay Movement,* Twayne, New York.

Adkins, Lisa (1995) *Gendered Work: Sexuality, Family and the Labour Market,* Open University Press, Buckingham.

Altman, Dennis (1982) *The Homosexualization of America, The Americanization of the Homosexual,* St Martin's Press, New York.

Altman, Dennis (1994) *Power and Community: Organizational and Cultural Responses to AIDS,* Taylor and Francis, London and Bristol, Pa.

Altman, Dennis (2001) *Global Sex,* University of Chicago Press, Chicago.

Amos, Valerie and Pratibha Parmar (1984) 'Challenging imperial feminism', *Feminist Review,* **17**.

Annan, Kofi (2003) 'To save Africa, we must save Africa's women', The Independent (London) 1 January p. 10.

Anthias, Floya and Nira Yuval Davis (1983) 'Contextualizing feminism – gender, ethic and class divisions', *Feminist Review* No. 15, Winter.

Anthias, Floya and Nira Yuval Davis (1993) *Racialized Boundaries: Race, Nation, Gender, Colour and Class and the anti-Racist Struggle,* Routledge, London and New York.

Archer, John and Barbara Lloyd (1982) *Sex and Gender,* Penguin, Harmondsworth.

Archer, John and Barbara Lloyd (2002) *Sex and Gender,* second edition, Cambridge University Press, Cambridge.

Argyle, Michael and Monika Henderson (1985) *The Anatomy of Relationships,* Heinemann, London.

Barr, R. F. *et al.* (1984) 'Homosexuality and psychological adjustment', *The Medical Journal of Australia,* **1**.

Bayer, Ronald (1981) *Homosexuality and American Psychiatry. The Politics of Diagnosis,* Basis Books, New York.

Beck, Ulrich and Elisabeth Beck-Gernsheim (1995) *The Normal Chaos of Love,* Polity Press, Cambridge.

Bell, Alan P., Martin S. Weinberg and Sue Keifer Hammersmith (1981) *Sexual Preference. Its Development in Men And Women,* Indiana University Press, Bloomington.

Bell, David and Gill Valentine (eds) (1995) *Mapping Desire*, Routledge, London and New York.

Bell, Mark (1998) 'Sexual Orientation and anti-Discrimination Policy: The European Community', in Terrell Carver and Veronique Mottier (eds) *Politics of Sexuality: Identity, Gender, Citizenship*, Routledge, London and New York.

Benedict, Ruth (1980, first published 1935) *Patterns of Culture*, Routledge & Kegan Paul, London.

Benjamin, Jessica (1984) 'Master and slave. The fantasy of erotic domination', in Ann Snitow, Christine Stansell and Sharon Thompson (eds), *Desire: The Politics of Sexuality*, Virago, London.

Bhatt, Chetan (1997) *Liberation and Purity: Race. New Religious Movements and the Ethics of Postmodernity*, UCL Press, London.

Boswell, John (1994) *Same Sex Unions in Pre-modern Europe*, Villard Books, New York.

Bouhdiba, Abdelwahab (1985) *Sexuality in Islam,* trans. Alan Sheridan, Routledge & Kegan Paul, London.

Bray, Alan (1982) *Homosexuality in Renaissance England,* Gay Men's Press, London.

Bullough, Vern L. (1976) *Sex, Society and History*, Science History Publications, New York. the particular essay, 'Sex in history: a virgin field', was first published in 1972.

Butler, Judith (1990) *Gender Trouble: Feminism and the Subversion of Identity*, Routledge, New York and London.

Butler, Judith (1993) *Bodies that Matter: On the Discursive Limits of Sex*, Routledge, New York and London.

Butt, Ronald 1985 'Lloyd George knew his followers', *The Times* (London), 19 September.

Califia, Pat (1979) 'Unraveling the sexual fringe. A secret side of lesbian sexuality', *The Advocate,* 27 Dec.

Cartledge, Sue (1983) 'Duty and desire: creating a feminist morality' in Sue, Cartledge and Joanna Ryan (eds), *Sex and Love. New Thoughts on Old Contradictions*, The Women's Press, London.

Cartledge, Sue and Joanna Ryan (eds) (1983) *Sex and Love. New Thoughts on Old Contradictions*, The Women's Press, London.

Chasseguet-Smirgel, Janine (1985) *Creativity and Perversion*, Free Association Books, London.

Cherfas, Jeremy and John Gribbin (1984) *The Redundant Male*, The Bodley Head, London.

Chodorow, Nancy (1980) 'Gender, relation and difference in psycho-analytic perspective', in Hester Eisenstein and Alice Jardine (eds), *The Future of Difference,* G. K. Hall, Boston, Mass.

Connell, R. W. (1995) *Masculinities*, Polity Press, Cambridge.

Connell, R. W. (2002) *Gender*, Polity Press, Cambridge

Coveney, L. *et al.* (1984) *The Sexuality Papers. Male Sexuality and the Social Control of Women*, Hutchinson, London.

Coward, Rosalind (1983) *Patriarchal Precedents: Sexuality and Social Relations*, Routledge & Kegan Paul, London.

Coward, Rosalind (1984) *Female Desire. Women's Sexuality Today*, Paladin, London.

Davis, Murray S. (1983) *Smut: Erotic Reality/Obscene Ideology*, University of Chicago Press, Chicago and London.

Dawkins, Richard (1978) *The Selfish Gene*, Granada, St Albans.

Wilson, E. O. (1978) *On Human Nature*, Harvard University Press, Cambridge, Mass.

D'Emilio, John (1983) *Sexual Politics, Sexual Communities. The Making of a Homosexual Minority in the United States 1940–1970*, University of Chicago Press, Chicago, London.

Dollimore, Jonathan (1991) *Sexual Dissidence: Augustine to Wilde, Freud to Foucault*, Clarendon Press, Oxford.

Duggan, Lisa, and Nan D. Hunter (1995) *Sex Wars: Sexual Dissent and Political Culture*, Routledge, New York and London.

Dyer, Richard (1985) 'Male sexuality in the media', in Andy Metcalf and Martin Humphries, *The Sexuality of Men,* Pluto Press, London.

Eardley, Tony (1985) 'Violence and sexuality' in Andy Metcalf and Martin Humphries, *The Sexuality of Men*, Pluto Press, London.

Edholm, F. (1982) 'The unnatural family', in Elizabeth Whitelegg *et al., The Changing Experience of Women,* Martin Robertson, Oxford.

Ellis, Havelock (1946; first published 1933) *The Psychology of Sex,* William Heinemann, London.

Epstein, Steven (1996) *Impure Science: AIDS, Activism and the Politics of Knowledge*, University of California Press, Berkeley.

Evans, David (1985) *Sexual Citizenship: The Material Construction of Sexualities*, Routledge, London and New York.

Eysenck, H. J. and G. D. Wilson (1979) *The Psychology of Sex,* Dent, London.

Faderman, Lillian (1981) *Surpassing the Love of Men,* Junction Books, London.

Flandrin, Jean-Louis (1985) 'Sex in married life in the early Middle Ages: the Church's teaching and behavioural reality', in Philippe Aries and Andre Bejin (eds) *Western Sexuality: Practice and Precept in Past and Present Times*, Blackwell, Oxford.

Ford, C. S. and F. A. Beach (1965; first published 1952) *Patterns of Sexual Behavior*, Methuen, London.

Foucault, Michel (1979) *The History of Sexuality, Vol. 1. An Introduction*, trans. Robert Hurley, Allen Lane, London.

Foucault, Michel (1980) *Power/Knowledge*, edited by Colin Gordon, Harvester Press, Brighton.

Foucault, Michel (1982/83) 'Sexual choice, sexual acts', *Salmagundi* **58–59**, 12.

Foucault, Michel (1984) 'On the genealogy of ethics: an overview of work in progress', in Paul Rabinow (ed.), *The Foucault Reader*, Pantheon Books, New York.

Foucault, Michel (1985) *The History of Sexuality, Vol. 2, The Use of Pleasure*, Viking, London.

Foucault, Michel (1986) *The History of Sexuality, Vol. 3, The Care of the Self*, Viking, London.

Freeman, Derek (1983) *Margaret Mead and Samoa. The Making and Unmaking of an Anthroppological Myth*, Harvard University Press, Cambridge, Mass., and London.

Freud, Ernst (ed.) (1961) *Letters of Sigmund Freud 1873–1939*, Hogarth Press, London.

Freud, Sigmund (1905) *Three Essays on the Theory of Sexuality* in Freud 1953–74, Vol. 7.

Freud, Sigmund (1910) *Leonardo da Vinci and a Memory of his Childhood*, in Freud 1953–74, Vol. 11.

Freud, Sigmund (1916–17) *Introductory Lectures on Psychoanalysis*, in Freud 1953–74, Vol. 16.

Freud, Sigmund (1920) *The Psychogenesis of Homosexuality in a Woman*, in Freud 1953–74, Vol. 18.

Freud, Sigmund (1921) *Group Psychology and the Analysis of the Ego*, in Freud 1953–74, Vol. 18.

Freud, Sigmund (1930) *Civilisation and its Discontents*, in Freud 1953–74, Vol. 21.

Freud, Sigmund (1953–74) *The Standard Edition of the Complete Psychological Works of Sigmund Freud*, ed. James Strachey, Hogarth Press and The Institute of Psychoanalysis, London.

Gagnon, John H. (1977) *Human Sexualities*, Scott, Foresman and Co., Glenview, Illinois.

Gagnon, John. H. and William Simon (1973) *Sexual Conduct. The Social Sources of Human Sexuality*, Hutchinson, London (1973).

Giddens, Anthony (1992) *The Transformation of Intimacy: Sexuality, Love and Eroticism in Modern Societies*, Polity Press, Cambridge.

Gilder, George F. (1973) *Sexual Suicide*, Quadrangle, New York.

Gittins, Diana (1982) *Fair Sex: Family Size and Structure 1900–1939*, Hutchinson, London.

Gouldner, Alvin (1973) *For Sociology*, Allen Lane, London.

Hall, Stuart (1980) 'Reformism and the legislation of consent', in National Deviancy Conference (ed.), *Permissiveness and Control. The Fate of the Sixties Legislation*, Macmillan, London.

Halperin, David M. (1990) *One Hundred Years of Homosexuality. And Other Essays on Greek Love*, Routledge, London. and New York.

Halperin, David M. (2002) *How to Do the History of Homosexuality* University of Chicago Press, Chicago.

Hamer, Dean *et al.* (1993) 'A linkage between DNA markers on the X chromosome and male sexual orientation', *Science*, **261**, 421–7.

Haour-Knipe, Mary, and Richard Rector (eds) (1996) *Crossing Borders: Migrations, Ethnicity and AIDS*, Taylor and Francis, London and Bristol, Pa.

Hearn, Jeff, Deborah L. Sheppard, Peta Tancred-Sheriff and Gibson Burrell (eds) (1989) *The Sexuality of Organization*, Sage, London, Newbury Park, New Delhi.

Heath, Stephen (1982) *The Sexual Fix*, Macmillan, London.

Herdt, Gilbert (1994) *Third Sex, Third Gender: Beyond Sexual Dimorphism in Culture and History*, Zone Books, New York.

Herman, Didi (1997) *The Anti Gay Agenda: Orthodox Vision and the Christian Right*, University of Chicago Press, Chicago.

Hirschfeld, Magnus (1930) 'Presidential address: The development and scope of sexology', in Norman Haire (ed.), *World League for Sexual Reform: Proceedings of the Third Congress*, London.

Holland, Janet, Caroline Ramazanoglu, Sue Sharpe and Rachel Thomson (1998) *The Male in the Head*, The Tufnell Press, London.

Home Office, Scottish Home Department (1957) *Report of the Committee on Homosexual Offences and Prostitution*, Cmnd 247, Her Majesty's Stationery Office, London.

Ignatieff, Michael (1984) *The Needs of Strangers*, Chatto & Windus, London.

Jackson, Stevi (2000) *Heterosexuality in Question*, Sage, London.

Jamieson, Lynn (1998) *Intimacy: Personal Relationships in Modern Societies*, Polity Press, Cambridge.

Johnson, Anne M., Catherine H. Mercer, Bob Erens *et al.* (2001) 'Sexual behaviour in Britain: partnerships, practices, and HIV risk behaviours', *The Lancet*, **358** (9296), 1835–42.

Jones, Ernest (1955) *The Life and Work of Sigmund Freud*, Vol. 2, Basic Books, New York.

Jones, Steve (2002) *Y: The Descent of Men*, Little, Brown, London.

Katz, Jonathan Ned (1995) *The Invention of Heterosexuality*, NAL/ Dutton, New York.

Kinsey, Alfred C., Wardell B. Pomeroy and Clyde E. Martin (1948) *Sexual Behavior in the Human Male*, W. B. Saunders, Philadelphia and London.

Kinsey, Alfred C., Wardell P. Pomeroy, Clyde E. Martin and Paul H. Gebhard (1953) *Sexual Behavior in the Human Female*, W. B. Saunders Company, Philadelphia and London.

Laplanche, J. and J. B. Pontalis (1980) *The Language of Psychoanalysis*, The Hogarth Press and the Institute of Psychoanalysis, London.

Laqueur, Thomas (1990) *Making Sex: Body and Gender from the Greeks to Freud*, Harvard University Press, Cambridge, Mass., and London.

Laumann, Edward O., Robert T. Michael, John H. Gagnon and S. Michaels (1994) *The Social Organization of Sexuality: Sexual Practices in the United States*, University of Chicago Press, Chicago.

Lauretis, Teresa de (1994) *Practice of Love: Lesbian Sexuality and Perverse Desire*, Indiana University Press, Bloomington and Idianopolis.

LeVay, Simon (1991) 'A difference in hypothalamic structure between hetrosexual and homosexual men', *Science*, **253**, 1034–7.

Linden, Robin Ruth *et al.* (eds) (1982) *Against Sadomasochism. A Radical Feminist Analysis*, Frog in the Web, East Palo Alto, Ca.

Loseke, D. R. *et al.* (2003) 'Forum: The Catholic Church, Paedophiles and Child Sex Abuse' in *Sexualities* **6** (1), 6–64.

Lowe, Donald M. (1982) *History of Bourgeois Perception*, Chicago University Press, Chicago.

Malinowski, Bronislaw (1929) *The Sexual Life of Savages*, Routledge & Kegan Paul, London.

Malinowski, Bronislaw (1963) *Sex, Culture and Myth*, Rupert Hart-Davis, London.

Masters, William H. and Virginia E. Johnson (1966) *Human Sexual Response*, Litte, Brown and Co., Boston.

McLaren, Angus (1978) *Birth Control in Nineteenth Century England*, Croom Helm, London.

McLaren, Angus (1984) *Reproductive Rituals*, Methuen, London.

Mead, Margaret (1948) *Sex and Temperament in Three Primitive Societies*, Routledge & Kegan Paul, London.

Mead, Margaret (1949) *Male and Female. A Study of the Sexes in a Changing World*, Victor Gollancz, London.

Mead, Margaret (1977; first published 1928) *Coming of Age in Samoa. A Study of Adolescence and Sex in Primitive Societies*, Penguin, Harmondsworth.

Messenger, J. C. (1971) 'Sex and repression in an Irish folk community', in D. S. Marshall and R. C. Suggs, *Human Sexual Behavior: Variations across the Ethnographic Spectrum*, Basic Books, London.

Mitchell, Juliet (1974) *Psychoanalysis and Feminism*, Allen Lane, London.

Moatti, Jean-Paul, Yves Souteyrand, Annice Prieur, Theo Sandfort and Peter Aggleton (2000) *AIDS in Europe: New Challenges for the Social Sciences*, Routledge, London and New York.

Moberly, Elizabeth R. (1983) *Psychoanalysis. The Early Development of Gender-identity*, Routledge & Kegan Paul, London.

Money, John (1980) *Love and Love Sickness*, Johns Hopkins University Press, Baltimore and London.

Neale, Palenta R. (1998) 'Sexuality and the International Conference on Population and Development. The Catholic Church in International Politics', in Terrell Carver and Veronique Mottier (eds) *Politics of Sexuality: Identity, Gender, Citizenship*, Routledge, London and New York.

Nicholson, John (1984) *Men and Women. How Different Are They?* Oxford University Press, Oxford and New York.

O'Carroll, Tom (1980) Paedophilia. The Radical Case, Peter Owen, London.

O'Connell Davidson, Julia (1998) *Prostitution, Power and Freedom*, Polity Press, Cambridge.

Oosterhuis, Harry (2000) *Stepchildren of Nature: Krafft-Ebing, Psychiatry and the Making of Sexual Identity*, University of Chicago Press, Chicago and London.

Ormolade, Barbara (1984) 'Hearts of darkness', in Ann Snitow, Christine Stansell and Sharon Thompson (eds), *Desire: The Politics of Sexuality*, Virago, London.

Padgug, Robert A. (1979) 'Sexual matters: on conceptualizing sexuality in history', *Radical History Review*, No. 20 Spring/Summer (special issue on 'Sexuality in History').

Parker, Richard (1991) *Bodies, Pleasures and Passions: Sexual Culture in Contemporary Brazil*, Beacon Press, Boston.

Parker, Richard (1999) *Beneath the Equator: Cultures of Desire, Male Homosexuality and emerging Gay Communities in Brazil*, Routledge, London and New York.

Parker, Richard, Marie Barbosa and Peter Aggleton (2000) *Framing the Sexual Subject: The Politics of Gender, Sexuality and Power*, University of California Press, Berkeley, Los Angeles and London.

Petchesky, Rosalind, and Karen Judd (1998) *Negotiating Reproductive Rights: Women's Perspectives across Countries and Cultures*, Zed Books, London.

Phillips, Kim M. and Barry Reay (eds) (2002) *Sexualities in History: A Reader*, Routledge, New York and London.

Plummer, Kenneth (1975) *Sexual Stigma. An Interactionist Account*, Routledge & Kegan Paul, London.

Plummer, Kenneth (ed.) (1980) *The Making of the Modern Homosexual,* Hutchinson, London.

ᚱ Plummer, Ken (1981) 'The paedophile's progress', in Brian Taylor (ed.), *Perspectives on Paedophilia,* Batsford, London.

Plummer, Kenneth (1984) 'Sexual diversity: a sociological perspective', in K. Howells (ed.), *Sexual Diversity,* Blackwell, Oxford.

Plummer, Ken (1995) *Telling Sexual Stories: Power, Change and Social Worlds,* Routledge, London and New York.

Plummer, Ken (2002) 'The square of intimate citizenship', *Citizenship Studies,* **5** (3), 237–53.

Pomeroy, Wardell, B. (1972) *Dr Kinsey and the Institute for Sex Research,* Harper & Row, New York.

Rattray Taylor, Gordon (1953) *Sex in History,* Thames & Hudson, London.

Reavey, Paula and Sam Warner (eds) (2003) *New Feminist Stories of Child Sexual Abuse: Sexual Scripts and Dangerous Dialogues,* Routledge, London and New York.

Renvoize, Jean (1982) *Incest: A Family History,* Routledge & Kegan Paul, London.

Reynolds, Robert (2002) *From Camp to Queer: Remaking the Australian Homosexual,* Melbourne University Press, Melbourne.

Rich, Adrienne (1984) 'Compulsory heterosexuality and lesbian existence', in Ann Snitow, Christine Stansell and Sharon Thompson (eds), *Desire: The Politics of Sexuality,* Virago, London.

Riley, Denise (1983) *War in the Nursery. Theories of the Child and Mother,* Virago, London.

Rose, Hilary 'Gay brains, gay genes and feminist science theory', in Jeffrey Weeks and Janet Holland (eds) (1996) *Sexual Cultures: Communities, Values and Intimacy,* Macmillan, Basingstoke and London.

Rose, Hilary and Steven Rose (eds) (2001) *Alas, Poor Darwin: Arguments against Evolutionary Psychology,* Vintage Books, London.

Rose, Jacqueline (1986) *Sexuality in the Field of Vision,* Verso, London.

Rose, Steven, Leon J. Kamin and R. C. Lewontin (1984) *Not in our Genes. Biology, Ideology and Human Nature,* Penguin, Harmondsworth.

Ross, Ellen and Rayna Rapp (1984) 'Sex and society: a research note from social history and anthropology', in Ann Snitow, Christine Stansell and Sharon Thompson (eds), *Desire: The Politics of Sexuality,* Virago, London (USA edition published in 1983 as *Powers of Desire: The Politics of Sexuality,* Monthly Review Press, New York).

Rubin, Gayle (1984) 'Thinking sex: notes for a radical theory of the politics of sexuality', in Carole S. Vance (ed.), *Pleasure and Danger. Exploring Female Sexuality,* Routledge & Kegan Paul, Boston and London.

Sahlins, Marshall (1976) *The Use and Abuse of Biology: An Anthropological Critique of Sociobiology*, Tavistock, London.

Samois (ed.) (1982) *Coming to Power. Writings and Graphics on Lesbian S/M*, Samois, Berkeley, Ca.

Schur, Edwin (1980) *The Politics of Deviance: Stigma Contests and the Uses of Power*, Prentice-Hall, Englewood Cliffs, N.J.

Scruton, Roger (1983) 'The case against feminism', *The Observer*, 22 May.

Scruton, Roger (1986) *Sexual Desire: A Philosophical Investigation*, Weidenfeld and Nicolson, London.

Seabrook, Jeremy (2001) *Travels in the Skin Trade: Tourism and the Sex Industry*, Pluto Press, London.

Segal, Lynne (1983) 'Sensual uncertainty, or why the clitoris is not enough', in Sue Cartledge and Joanna Ryan (eds), *Sex and Love. New Thoughts on Old Contradictions*, The Women's Press, London.

Segal, Lynne (1994) *Straight Sex: The Politics of Pleasure*, Virago, London.

Segal, Lynne (1998) 'Only the literal: the contradictions of anti-pornography feminism', *Sexualities*, 1(1), 43–62.

Segal, Lynne (1999) *Why Feminism?*, Polity Press, Cambridge.

Silva, Elizabeth and Carol Smart (eds) (1999) *The 'New' Family?* Sage, London, Thousand Oaks, New Delhi.

Simon, William (1996) *Postmodern Sexualities*, Routledge, London and New York.

Singer, Irving (1973) *The Goals of Human Sexuality*, Wildwood House, London.

Snitow, Ann, Christine Stansell and Sharon Thompson (eds) (1983) *Desire: The Politics of Sexuality*, Virago, London.

Socarides, C. W. (1978) *Homosexuality*, Jason Aranson, New York.

Sontag, Susan (1983) *Illness as Metaphor*, Penguin, Harmondsworth.

Sontag, Susan (1989) *AIDS and its Metaphors*, Allen Lane, London.

Stein, Edward (ed.) (1992) *Forms of Desire: Sexual Orientation and the Social Construction Controversy*, Routledge, New York and London.

Stoller, Robert J. (1977) *Perversion. The Erotic Form of Hatred*, Quartet, London.

Stoler, Ann Laura (1995) *Race and the Education of Desire: Foucault's History of Sexuality and the Colonial Order of Things*, Duke University Press, Durham, N.C., and London.

Stone, Lawrence (1977) *The Family, Sex and Marriage in England 1500–1800*, Weidenfeld & Nicolson, London.

Symons, Donald (1979) *The Evolution of Human Sexuality*, Oxford University Press, Oxford and New York.

Taylor, Brian (1981) 'Introduction' in Brian Taylor (ed.), *Perspectives on Paedophilia*, Batsford, London.

Thompson, Bill (1994) *Sadomasochism: Painful Perversion or Pleasurable Play?*, Cassell, London.

Thornhill, Randy and Craig Palmer (2000) *A Natural History of Rape: Biological Bases of Sexual Coercion*, MIT Press, Cambridge, Mass.

Vance, Carole S. (1984) Pleasure and danger: towards a politics of sexuality', in Carole S. Vance (ed.), *Pleasure and Danger. Exploring Female Sexuality*, Routledge & Kegan Paul, Boston and London.

Veyne, Paul (1985) 'Homosexuality in ancient Rome', in Philippe Aries and Andre Bejin (eds.), *Western Sexuality: Practice and Precept in Past and Present Times*, Blackwell, Oxford.

Warner, Michael (1993) *Fear of a Queer Planet: Queer Politics and Social Theory*, University of Minnesota Press, Minneapolis and London.

Warnock, Mary (1985) A *Question of Life. The Warnock Report on Human Fertilisation and Embryology*, Basil Blackwell, Oxford.

Weeks, J. (1977) *Coming Out. Homosexual Politics in Britain from the 19th Century to the Present*, Quartet, London.

Weeks, Jeffrey (1985) *Sexuality and its Discontents. Meanings, Myths and Modern Sexualities*, Routledge & Kegan Paul, London.

Weeks, Jeffrey (1989; first published 1981) *Sex , Politics and Society: The Regulation of Sexuality since 1800*, Longman, Harlow.

Weeks, Jeffrey (1995) *Invented Moralities: Sexual Values in an Age of Uncertainty*, Polity Press, Cambridge.

Weeks, Jeffrey (1998) 'The sexual citizen', *Theory, Culture and Society*, **15**, (3–4), 35–52.

Weeks, Jeffrey (2000) *Making Sexual History*, Polity Press, Cambridge.

Weeks, Jeffrey, Brian Heaphy and Catherine Donovan (2001) *Same Sex Intimacies: Families of Choice and other Life Experiments*, Routledge, London and New York.

Weeks, Jeffrey, Janet Holland and Matthew Waites (eds) (2003) *Sexualities and Society: A Reader*, Polity Press, Cambridge.

Weinberg, Thomas and G. W. Levi Kamel (eds) (1983) S *and M. Studies in Sado Masochism,* Prometheus Books, Buffalo, N.Y.

Weinstein, Fred and Gerald M. Platt (1969) *The Wish to be Free. Psyche and Value Change,* University of California Press, Berkeley.

Wellings, Kaye, Julia Field, Anne M. Johnson and J. Wadsworth (1994) *Sexual Behaviour in Britain: The National Survey of Sexual Attitudes and Lifestyles*, Macmillan, London and Basingstoke.

Weston, Kath (1991) *Families We Choose: Lesbians, Gays, Kinship*, Colombia University Press, New York.

Williams, Raymond (1983) *Keywords. A Vocabulary of Culture and Society*, Flamingo, London.

Wilson, E. O. (1975) *Sociobiology: The New Synthesis,* Harvard University Press, Cambridge, Mass., and London.

Wilson, E. O. (1978) *On Human Nature*, Harvard University Press, Cambridge, Mass.

Wintermute, Robert and Mads Andenaes (eds) (2001) *Legal Recognition of Same-Sex Partnerships*, Hart Publishing, Oxford and Portland, Oregon.

Witz, Anne, Susan Halford and Mike Savage (1996) 'Organized Bodies: Gender, Sexuality, and Embodiment', in Lisa Adkins and Vicki Merchant, eds, *Sexualizing the Social. Power and the Organization of Sexuality*, Macmillan, Basingstoke and London.

Wolmark, Jenny (ed.) (1999) *Cybersexualities: A Reader in Feminist Theory, Cyborgs and Cyberspace*, Edinburgh University Press, Edinburgh.

INDEX